God's Mighty Hands/ Outstretched Arm

God's Power and Plan for the World

KENNETH L. SHERLOCK

A MIGHTY HAND AND AN OUTSTRETCHED ARM

GOD'S PLAN AND POWER AT WORK IN THE WORLD

BY

KENNETH L. SHERLOCK

Deuteronomy 26:8 "And the Lord brought us out of Egypt with a mighty hand and an outstretched arm."

ARPress
45 Dan Road Suite 5
Canton MA 02021

| Hotline: | 1(888) 821-0229 |
| Fax: | 1(508) 545-7580 |

Ordering Information:

Quantity sales. Special discounts are available on quantity purchases by corporations, associations, and others. For details, contact the publisher at the address above.

Printed in the United States of America.

| ISBN-13: | Softcover | 979-8-89389-315-1 |
| | eBook | 979-8-89389-314-4 |

Library of Congress Control Number: 2024916143

TABLE OF CONTENTS

Dedicated to my son, Michael, who left this earth way too early.

INTRODUCTION

My wife is a list-maker. I am not. Her idea of starting the day is to make a list of the things she has to do. I never make a list. I go through the day, flitting from one thing to another and usually manage to accomplish something productive.

We have been married for over 37 years and have influenced one another in many ways. I have encouraged her to be more spontaneous and enjoy things that are not on her list. She has encouraged me to be more careful in planning for future events.

As soon as I graduated from high school, I left home. I lived each day as it came and had no plan for the future.

The capstone of my "non-planning" happened a short time before I met my wife. I decided to make the 275-mile trip to see my parents. My tires were bad but I started out. anyway. Normally it is a five-hour trip. When I got to a town fifty miles down the road, I discovered I had a low tire.

I started to get out my spare and found it was flat. It was night and nothing was open. I decided to stay there that night and get the tire fixed in the morning. I got the tire fixed and the spare fixed and I was on my way. Two miles out of town, I had another flat. That was when I discovered that I had no jack. Fortunately, God was watching over me and someone came along and gave me a jack. Before I got back home, I had a total of five flat tires. This was the turning point in convincing me that maybe I ought to give some thought to my activities. DUH! You think? I'm glad to say, I have experienced some growth in the area of planning ahead.

Unlike me, God had a plan for the people he created. Ephesians 1:4 lets us know that God had it all planned out, even before the beginning of creation. He knew, before He planted that first tree, that it would one day be cut down and made into a cross upon which His Son would pay the penalty for the sin of mankind.

The Bible is a mysterious book to many people. They may know in a general way what the Bible says, but have no idea how it fits together. The purpose of this brief study is to show God's orderly plan from beginning to end. That plan hinges on God's relationship with mankind.

Chapter 1 tells of a perfect creation and how sin ruined that perfect relationship with God. Many years later, after the flood, God chose one man, Abraham, and called him to follow Him. Abraham is the subject of chapter 2.

Chapter 3 tells about how God fulfills His purpose in spite of man's sinfulness. Jacob's son, Joseph, was sold into slavery in Egypt. Through many hardships and disappointments, Joseph became second in command of the nation of Egypt. Thus, he was in a perfect place to sustain his family through a period of drought.

Chapters 4 and 5 show God's dealings with Abraham's descendants who had become a nation known as Israel. We see how God redeemed them from slavery, led them into the wilderness and gave them laws to live by. He not only gave them laws but gave them a system of worship.

It had been God's purpose all along to give His people a land of their own. Chapter 6 tells of a lack of faith that caused the Israelites to lose out on God's blessings. What was a failure for that generation became a victory for the next generation. Chapter 7 shows how God fulfilled his divine promise. A new leader was chosen and a new land was conquered.

Chapters 8 through 11 cover the events that happen after the people were in the promised land. God warned them of discipline if they remained disobedient to Him. The first of the Ten Commandments was, basically, to make Him number 1 in their lives. If He was number one, they wouldn't be tempted to have anything to do with other so-called "gods." Not many years after entering the land, they started worshipping the false "gods" that the Canaanites worshipped. God sent prophet after prophet to warn them that this false worship would bring about the loss of the blessings God wanted them to have. We see that disobedience caused discipline. Discipline brought about repentance. Repentance brought about a restoration of blessings.

Chapter 12 tells of the exciting time in history when God actually entered the human race. Chapter 13 tells us how to respond to that truth – how to make it personal.

The subject of chapter 14 is both painful and hopeful. It speaks of a shameful death but a glorious resurrection and a living hope for us.

Chapter 15 deals with the spread of the church as recorded in the book of Acts. Jesus told His disciples that they would do greater things than He did and the book of Acts records some of these things.

Chapter 16 deals with this present period of time we call the church age. We will see how various Christian leaders wrote letters to the churches that were established. They wrote to encourage them, rebuke them on some points and instruct them on how to live out the grace of God in their daily lives. The apostle Paul also wrote to individuals such as Timothy, Titus and a man called Philemon.

Finally, we come to the part we've all been waiting for! How is it all going to turn out? This is the subject of chapter 17. Guess what – God wins!

Come with me and follow along as we see the awesome plan and power of God from beginning to end.

Chapter 1

THE BEGINNING OF THE STORY

Genesis 1:1 In the beginning God created the heavens and the earth.

Genesis 1:26 & 27: Then God said, "Let us make man in our image, in our likeness and let them rule over the fish of the sea the birds of the air, over the livestock, over all the earth, and over all the creatures that move along the ground." So, God created man in His own image, in the image of God He created him; male and female, He created them.

A PERFECT BEGINNING

The Bible begins with a clear statement. There was a specific time when God began the creation of the world. It is stated as a fact, not a theory. For thousands of years people had no problem with that fact. Gradually, people began to question this fact and began to believe that maybe God did not create the world, after all.

In 1831 Charles Darwin set off on a five-year voyage of exploration. He observed numerous animals and plants. Because of the variations he observed he became convinced that species were not fixed categories, as was commonly supposed, but were capable of variation. He finished the voyage in 1836 and devoted his time to more study. In 1859 he published the well-known "Origin Of The Species".

Granted, Darwin did not say that God did not create the world. Neither did he say anything about human beings evolving from a lower life form. Nevertheless, thoughts about the world around us began to change. Fast forward to today where the idea of a world that is only 6,000 years old is mocked, ridiculed and vigorously denied.

How do we get the figure 6,000? The Bible gives us a very careful account of ages in the book of Genesis. Adding these all up, we find that Abraham was born about 2,000 years after Adam. There was another 2,000 years until Christ came. Add 2,000 more years and you get 6,000.

It all boils down to the question, "Can we trust the Word of God to be accurate, or not?" If chapters 1 & 2 of Genesis are not accurate then we can't trust any of the rest of the Bible. Since we weren't there at the beginning, we have to take somebody's word for it. I take my stand on God's word.

God's power is shown in creation.

All God had to do was say the word and it was done. The phrase, "And God said…" is repeated eight times in Genesis 1. God's power is evident, not only in creation, but all through the Bible. Pharaoh in Egypt asked the question, "Who is God, that I should worship Him?" In response to that question God revealed His power through a series of ten plagues on the land of Egypt. The final show of power was the parting of the Red Sea where the Israelites had a clear path to freedom and the Egyptians were destroyed.

We, today, are impressed by power. You will be happy to know that God has not lost any of His power. I have experienced that power when God changed the direction of my life. That is what enables me to believe in a God that is capable of creating a world in six days.

God's wisdom is shown in creation.

God is a God of order and organization. As God created the world, each thing He created was the springboard for further creation.

The first thing God created was light. Keep in mind that this was three days before the sun and moon were created. After He created the light, He made a division between heaven and earth. Seas and dry land were created, and vegetation covered the dry land.

See how the dry land was being prepared for the animals and human beings who would inhabit it. The next day God set the sun and moon and stars in place.

Finally, it was time for birds to live in the trees that had been created and the marine life to inhabit the seas. Now came the animals that could take advantage of the vegetation on the earth.

Then came the final act of creation – human beings, created in the image of God.

God's wisdom is further shown in the way He dealt with Adam. He gave him a job to do and gave him a custom-made companion. One more thing He gave Adam is a restriction. Genesis 2:16 and 17 states, *"And the Lord God commanded the man, saying, 'You may surely eat of every tree of the garden, but of the tree of the knowledge of good and evil you shall not eat, for in the day that you eat of it you shall surely die.' "*

Psalm 104 speaks of the power and wisdom of our mighty creator. He provides water for the beasts of the earth, trees for the birds to nest in, plants for man to cultivate. He is so wise that He arranges for beasts of prey to have a different time schedule from mankind.

God's desire for a relationship is seen in the creation of man.

God made everything by speaking the word. Genesis 1:26 shows that the creation of human beings was a specific act that was thought out beforehand. Verse 26 tells us what God was about to do. He was going to create mankind in His own image and give him authority over all other created beings (except for cats, of course!)

Chapter 2 of Genesis does not contradict chapter 1 but goes into more detail. Adam is created, gives names to the animals that come to him, Eve is created, and the first marriage ceremony is performed. So far so good. They have perfect fellowship with one another and perfect fellowship with God.

A POOR CHOICE Genesis 2:15-17 and 3:6 & 7

There was only one prohibition.

There they were in a perfect environment and there was only one restriction. Perhaps you think if it was *you* in that situation, you wouldn't mess it up like Eve did. I doubt it. Our tendency as a human being is to do the thing we are forbidden to do. If we see a sign saying, "Keep off the grass" we walk across that grass. How about a "wet paint" sign? Who can resist touching it to see if it, indeed, is really wet?

Why did God establish that one restriction? Could it be that He wanted man to have a choice? Part of love is obedience. If there were no restrictions, the first couple would love Him and have fellowship with Him because they had no choice. We want our kids to love us, not because they have to, but because they choose to. I believe God is the same way. He gives us free will and lets us choose whether to love Him or spurn Him.

Satan influenced the woman but did not cause her to sin.

Eve chose to listen to the lies of Satan. There was a comedian named Flip Wilson years ago whose favorite line was, "The devil made me do it." It got a lot of laughs, but it is not the truth. Satan cannot make us do anything.

The devil cast doubt upon the word of God. "Did God really say…?" Then the devil cast doubt upon the goodness of God. He implied that God was holding something back from them. The final step was when he stated flatly that God did not really mean what He said. "You will not surely die!"

The woman not only sinned but persuaded her husband to sin as well.

One of the worst things about sin is that it is contagious. I hear people say, "I'm not hurting anybody else by my sin." Yes, you are! You are hurting the ones that love you and there is a good chance that they will end up copying your sin.

Now that sin had entered the picture, it changed the way they viewed each other. There was not that perfect fellowship between them anymore because when sin entered, so did guilt and shame.

THE CONSEQUENCES OF SIN Genesis 3:14-19 and 23 & 24

Good news! Sin can be forgiven. Bad news! Sin has consequences that are far-reaching. What are some of those consequences? Here are a few.

An increase in pain

Did you ever wonder how much less painful it would be to give birth to a child if Eve had not sinned? No wonder they call it labor!

An increase in labor.

Because the ground was now cursed it no longer yielded its produce abundantly and naturally. Now, there were weeds to choke out the life of the plants and thorns to pierce the hands of the laborer.

Banishment from the garden

Not only was there an increase in pain and an increase of labor, there was banishment from the perfect environment they had. Things could never be the way they were before sin.

This is the worst part of the whole sorry mess. They lost that perfect relationship with God. Now instead of welcoming His presence with them in the cool of the day, they hid from Him. Their love for Him was replaced by fear of Him.

This marred relationship has touched us all. Only in Jesus, the seed of the woman, can that relationship be restored. Yes, God forgave their sin and provided clothing for them. That clothing required the death of an animal. That first animal sacrifice was a picture of the One who was coming as the perfect lamb of God to take away the sins of the world.

Chapter 2

GOD CONTINUES THE STORY

Genesis 12:1 "The Lord had said to Abram, 'Leave your country, your people and your father's household and go to the land I will show you.' "

Genesis 15:6 "Abram believed the Lord and He credited to him as righteousness."

Genesis 3 tells of the first sin. Genesis 4 tells of the first murder. After a few generations, sin became so bad that God sent judgment in the form of a flood. From Noah's three sons God chose one man, Abram (later called Abraham), a descendant of Noah's son, Shem, to follow Him. His name, Abram, meant "exalted father". God later changed it to Abraham, which means "father of a multitude. Since he is more widely known as "Abraham, that is what we will call him throughout this chapter. (Except in the scripture quotations.)

ABRAHAM FOLLOWS GOD.

Abraham's family were idol worshippers but Abraham was about to be introduced to the true God. Instead of worshipping the moon and the stars, Abraham would be a follower of the one who created the moon and called the stars by name.

The Bible does not say how God appeared to Abraham. We can be sure, though, that Abraham knew that it was real and was faced with making a decision. We can see three things about following God that can carry over into our own lives.

It was God who issued the invitation.

Why did God choose Abraham? We could ask the same thing about why God chose Jacob over Esau while they were both still in the womb and had done nothing either good or bad. Why did God choose David over his older brothers? Could it be that God not only sees the heart but also knows the future? He saw something in Abraham that was different from the people around him. He saw a man who would respond to His leading.

For that matter, why did God choose me? Not everyone in my family feels the same way about the Lord that I do. In fact, some of them think I am crazy for believing as I do. When I think about their talents and abilities that are greater than mine, I thank God that He sees the heart. I was not very athletic as I was growing up. I soon got used to being the last or next-to-last being chosen for a team. That is why it really thrilled me that God deliberately chose me.

God promised to bless him.

God's promises to Abraham were specific. He promised to give his descendants a land of their own. God was going to show it to Abraham first. He promised to make him into a great nation who would be a blessing to all the people on the earth. This was fulfilled many years later at the birth of our Lord Jesus Christ who was a descendant of Abraham. Through Jesus, everyone in the world can receive the blessings of God. It doesn't matter what your race or background is. We are all equal at the foot of the cross.

God promised reward for obedience.

After Abraham obeyed and followed God to Canaan, God appeared to him at a place called Shechem. God said to him, *"To your offspring I will give this land."* (Genesis 12:7) This was quite a promise to a 75 year-old man who did not yet have a son. Does it pay to obey God? Absolutely. God still rewards obedience.

Keep in mind, however, the fact that Abraham only lived to see part of the promises fulfilled. He had to wait for 25 years before his son, Isaac, was born. His descendants did not receive the land God promised until many generations later. If we obey God, He will bless us, but we may not see those blessings at once.

ABRAHAM WORSHIPS GOD.

We, in the church today, talk a lot about worship. We call our church services "worship services". We label certain music "worship songs". We have different styles of worship. To some, to worship is to kneel, bow the head and be silent in awe of God. To others, worship is to stand with hands lifted to heaven and be loud in praise to God. Which is right? The answer – it is not the position of the body but the condition of the heart that makes the difference. The woman at the well asked Christ which mountain in Israel was the proper one on which to worship God. Jesus told her that God was a spirit and those who worshipped Him must worship in spirit and in truth. If we go to a church service and are unchanged by it, then we have not truly worshipped.

Worshipping God meant giving up his security.

Many people are kept from letting God have first place in their life because they are attached to their "things". Jesus admonished His followers to deny themselves, pick up their cross and follow Him. He didn't say, "Pick up your couch."

Jesus' disciples all had to leave the security of their jobs to follow Him. Peter and Andrew, James and John all had to leave their fishing boats. Matthew had to leave his tax booth. So, Abram, likewise, had to leave the security of a settled existence to become a wandering nomad.

Worshipping God meant venturing into the unknown.

It must have taken a great deal of faith for Abraham to start off on a journey to unknown territory. He was at an age where he could have been thinking of retirement instead of following God to a place he had never seen. Evidently, Abraham thought the rewards would be worth the risk. There is always a risk in following God, but the rewards are out of this world!

Worshipping God meant being obedient to God.

Jesus said, "If you love me, you will keep my commands." I had a son who was very loving to his mother and me but was not very good at being obedient. As God revealed Himself to Abraham little by little, Abraham was led to conclude that God was worthy of love, worthy of respect and worthy of obedience. Everywhere Abraham went he built an altar.

The law of Moses had not yet been put into effect, but Abraham knew that worshipping God involved an animal sacrifice. Building an altar was a deliberate act that required both time and effort.

ABRAHAM BELIEVES GOD.

Genesis 15:1-6 "After this, the word of the Lord came to Abram in a vision: 'Do not be afraid, Abram. I am your shield, your very great reward.' But Abram said, 'O sovereign Lord, what can you give me since I remain childless and the one who will inherit my estate is Eliezer of Damascus?' And Abram said, 'You have given me no children; so a servant in my household will be my heir.' He took him outside and said, 'Look up at the heavens and count the stars – if indeed you can count them.' Then He said to him, 'So shall your offspring be.' **Abram believed the Lord, and He credited to him as righteousness."** *(Emphasis mine.)*

By the time we come to the scripture quoted above Abraham had suffered from a lapse of faith when he went down to Egypt and tried to pass his wife off as his sister. He had also suffered the rupture of a relationship with his nephew, Lot. The above scripture shows that he was concerned about the lack of an heir to carry on the family name. In spite of these setbacks, verse 6 says that Abraham believed God.

He believed God in spite of circumstances.

Abraham could have looked at his circumstances and concluded that God had let him down. Instead, he had enough faith to look at the faithfulness of God rather than the futility of the present situation.

So many people today are crushed and bowed down by circumstances in their life. Faith is lifting our eyes to the God who can cause those circumstances to work for our good. See Romans 8:28.

Even though he had periods of doubt, Abraham's faith grew stronger day by day.

The more that Abraham experienced God's love and God's leadership, the stronger his faith grew. Every time God appeared to him and spoke to him, Abraham's wall of belief grew higher and higher. Eventually his faith would grow so strong that he could obey God's instructions even if it meant giving up the son he loved so much. See that story in Genesis 22. Abram's obedience in that situation prompted God to reward Abraham by providing a substitute sacrifice.

Believing God is what pleases Him.

Hebrews 11:6 "And without faith it is impossible to please God, because anyone who comes to Him must believe that He exists and that he rewards those who earnestly seek Him.

Nothing damages a relationship more than a lack of trust. If we are grieved by someone who does not trust us, imagine how much greater is God's grief. May it never be said that we grieved God by our lack of faith. Rather, let it be said that we brought joy to God by our faith.

God was so pleased with Abram's faith the He even gave him a new name. From "Abram", meaning "exalted father" he became "Abraham" which means "father of a multitude."

Chapter 3

GOD BRINGS BLESSING THROUGH A FLAWED FAMILY

Genesis 25:19-23 "This is the account of Abraham's son Isaac. Abraham became the father of Isaac, and Isaac was forty years old when he married Rebekah, daughter of Bethuel the Aramean from Paddan Aram and sister of Laban the Aramean. Isaac prayed to the Lord on behalf of his wife, because she was barren. The Lord answered his prayer, and his wife Rebekah became pregnant. The babies jostled each other within her, and she said, 'Why is this happening to me?' So she went to inquire of the Lord. The Lord said to her, 'Two nations are in your womb, and two peoples from within you will be separated; one people will be stronger than the other, and the older will serve the younger.' "

Genesis 28:1 & 2 "So Isaac called for Jacob and blessed him and commanded him: ' Do not marry a Canaanite woman. Go at once to Paddan Aram, to the house of your mother's father Bethuel. Take a wife for yourself from there, from among the daughters of Laban, your mother's brother.'

Although God had promised Abraham many descendants, it didn't look very promising for many years. Isaac was forty years old when he got married and Rebekah didn't get pregnant for twenty years. Isaac was sixty years old when two sons were born to him – Esau and Jacob.

At that time, it was customary for the oldest son to get a double portion of the inheritance. Esau was the oldest son, even if only by a few minutes. God, however, had told Rebekah that it was the younger son who would get the blessing.

As the boys grew up, their differences were evident and the difference among their parents became evident also. Isaac favored Esau and Rebekah favored Jacob.

One day, Jacob took advantage of Esau's hunger and offered to feed him in exchange for the birthright. Esau agreed to that arrangement, so the birthright was legally Jacob's.

Isaac very likely knew what God's plan was, but he was determined to give the blessing to HIS favorite son – Esau. Crafty Rebekah was just as determined that HER favorite son was to get the blessing. Instead of confronting her husband directly and reminding him of what God had said and reminding him that Esau had given up his birthright for a bowl of stew, she resorted to deception. She had Jacob impersonate Esau and receive the blessing.

What a family! We see strife between the brothers, favoritism by the parents, deception by Rebekah and disregard for God's will by Isaac.

Because of Jacob's deception, Esau held a grudge against him and Jacob fled to his mother's brother's home, many miles away. There he fell in love and worked seven years for a wife. The old saying, "What goes around comes around" came true for Jacob. He impersonated his brother years before and now Rachel's sister impersonated her. Jacob was tricked into marrying Rachel's sister, Leah. Since bigamy was not illegal in those days, Jacob married Rachel, too. So begins another dysfunctional family!

The sisters were always competing against one another for their husband's affection. One of the ways they thought they could earn his favor was by bearing sons. Since Rachel couldn't get pregnant, she gave her maidservant to Jacob as a wife. She would then adopt the children as her own. Soon, Leah did the same thing. Now instead of one wife (which was God's original plan), Jacob had four wives. What a mess! Can God really bring anything good out of this? Yes, He can! God is the only one who can bring anything good out of the mess we make of our lives.

Finally, Rachel's dream came true and she gave birth to a son named Joseph. She later gave birth to another son, Benjamin, and died shortly after giving birth to him.

Jacob, (whose name God changed to Israel, meaning "prince with God") was back in the land of Canaan with his twelve sons. These sons became the heads of the twelve tribes known as the Israelites. Genesis, chapter 37 is where the story of Joseph begins.

JOSEPH IS FAVORED.

Genesis 37:2-4 says, "…Joseph, a young man of seventeen, was tending the flocks with his brothers, the sons of Bilhah and the sons of Zilpah, his father's wives, and he brought his father a bad report about them. Now Israel loved Joseph more than any of his other sons, because he had been born to him in his old age; and he made a richly ornamented robe for him. When his brothers saw that their father loved him more than any of them, they hated him and could not speak a kind word to him."

Not only was Joseph the favorite, he was a tattletale. The tattling might have been enough to cause resentment, but hatred came because of the obvious favoritism.

What was Jacob thinking? Didn't he remember how he felt when he knew his own father favored Esau? Didn't he realize he was putting Joseph into danger? Didn't he see how unfair he was to his other sons?

The older ten sons were expected to work hard to take care of the flocks. How much work was Joseph expected to do in his fancy robe?

The Bible doesn't answer all these questions. In spite of Jacob's faulty thinking, God had a purpose in the feelings and emotions of the brothers. His purpose was to prepare the way for a future time of hardship – a time of famine.

God gave Joseph two dreams that seemed to hint that he would, at some time, be in a position of authority. First, he dreamed that they were binding sheaves of grain in the field. Suddenly his sheaf stood upright and the others bowed down to it. Second, he dreamed that the sun, moon, and eleven stars were bowing down to him.

When Joseph saw his brothers hated him, why did he make the matter worse by telling them the dream. Why didn't he just keep his mouth shut? Perhaps it was because he wanted to rub it in a little. Whatever the reason, it made his brothers hate him all the more.

JOSEPH IS FORSAKEN

While his brothers were off with the sheep and goats, Jacob asked Joseph to go check on them. They were not just down the road a couple of miles. They were at the town of Shechem – fifty miles away. When Joseph arrived there and found they had gone to Dothan, he walked the additional thirteen miles to do the job his father had given him to do.

We have observed Joseph's weaknesses. This episode reveals some of his strengths. He was obedient. He was willing to go farther than he had to go. He showed no animosity toward his brothers.

Genesis 37:18 & 19 says, *"But they saw him in the distance, and before he reached them, they plotted to kill him. 'Here comes that dreamer!' they said to each other."* The anger that had been seething in them all these years boiled over into murderous rage.

Reuben, the oldest brother, talked them into throwing him into a pit that was nearby. Reuben apparently had a little more mercy than the others. He was planning to come back and pull him out after they had gone their way.

They stripped him of his robe, threw him in the pit, and, callously sat down to eat their lunch. Just at that time the brothers spied a caravan of traders going down to Egypt. Judah persuaded them to sell Joseph instead of kill him. Genesis 37:26 & 27 says, *"Judah said to his brothers, 'what will we gain if we kill our brother and cover up his blood? Come, let's sell him to the Ishmaelites and not lay our hands on him; after all, he is our brother, our own flesh and blood.' His brothers agreed."* Then they planned to dip his coat in blood and let their father assume that Joseph had been killed by a wild animal.

Joseph may have thought that he was abandoned by his family and abandoned by his God, but God still had a plan. Chapter 39 of Genesis lets us know that God is still in the picture. Four times we find the words, "The Lord was with Joseph."

After rising to the level of top servant in his master's household, his world all came crashing down. His master's wife had a lustful eye upon him but he continually refused her advances. Finally, she got the chance to accuse him of attempted rape. Potiphar (his master) threw him into prison. Oh no! Just when things were going so well!

Even there, God was with him and gave him favor in the eyes of the warden. Pretty soon he was still a prisoner, but now he was the one in charge of the other prisoners.

Two of the prisoners were Pharaoh's cupbearer and his baker. Both of them had dreams, which Joseph interpreted. Joseph revealed that the dreams meant the baker was to lose his life, but the cupbearer was to get his job back. Joseph asked the cupbearer to put in a good word for him to Pharaoh. The cupbearer promised to do so, but promptly forgot him. Just when Joseph had a glimmer of hope, he found himself forsaken again by an empty promise.

JOSEPH IS FORGIVING

Two years later Pharaoh had two dreams. Finally, the cupbearer remembered Joseph. He was sent for and given the opportunity to interpret Pharaoh's dreams. The dreams were to warn him that there would be seven years of plenty in the land of Egypt, followed by seven years of severe famine.

Along with interpreting the dream, Joseph gave Pharaoh advice. He advised him to put someone in charge of storing up food during the years of plenty. Pharaoh was so pleased by this advice that he appointed Joseph as that man.

What a promotion! From prison to second in command of the land of Egypt! Now he was really in a position of authority. His character is revealed by what he did not do. He did not punish the woman who lied about him. He did not punish Potiphar for throwing him in prison. He did not punish the cupbearer for forgetting about him for two years.

Nine years later, after the years of plenty were over and the time of famine had begun, Joseph's brothers came down to Egypt to buy food. He pretended not to know them and accused them of being spies. They replied that they were not spies, but were the sons of one man.

One had died and the youngest one was still with their father. He told them that the only way they could prove it was to bring their youngest brother down with them. If they did not have him with them, they could not even buy food.

Jacob was reluctant to let Benjamin go with them but, facing starvation, eventually gave in. On their second trip, Joseph revealed himself to his brothers and invited them to come down and let him provide for them. Twenty-two years after the brothers sold Joseph, the family was reunited.

Many years later, after their father died, the brothers were scared Joseph was going to lower the boom on them and begged for forgiveness. Joseph's attitude toward them and toward God is shown in these verses. *Genesis 50:19 – 21 "But Joseph said to them, 'Don't be afraid. Am I in the place of God? You intended to harm me, but God intended it for good to accomplish what is now being done, the saving of many lives. So then, don't be afraid. I will provide for you and your children." And he reassured them and spoke kindly to them."*

Oh, that we could have an attitude like that toward the injustices of life! It doesn't matter what happened to me or who wronged me – God was in charge of it all!

The land of Egypt became a place of blessing and protection for many years. Joseph's brothers prospered and many children were born to them. Things were good for many years. All good things must come to an end, however. Suddenly a new Pharaoh came to the throne that did not know about Joseph and did not care for his family. Suddenly the place of blessing became a place of danger and misery.

Chapter 4

GOD DELIVERS HIS PEOPLE

Exodus 3:7 & 8 "The Lord said, 'I have indeed seen the misery of my people in Egypt. I have heard them crying out because of their slave drivers, and I am concerned about their suffering. So I have come down to rescue them from the hand of the Egyptians and to bring them up out of that land into a good and spacious land, a land flowing with milk and honey…'"

In Genesis, chapter 15 we find that God had made a covenant with Abraham. In making this agreement God let Abraham know that his descendants would be slaves in a country that was not their own for over 400 years. God promised Abraham many descendants and also promised to give them that land in which Abraham was now living. He was also letting Abraham know that the promise would not be fulfilled for many years.

God renewed these promises to Abraham's son, Isaac and to Isaac's son, Jacob. Just as God had promised, Jacob and his family went to live in a country that was not their own – the land of Egypt.

At first, the land of Egypt was a place of blessing and provision. They were welcomed and favored. As time went on, however, a new king of Egypt arose. This king feared them, enslaved them and endangered their lives. Finally, he went so far as to issue an order that all baby boys should be killed.

This is the situation that the baby, Moses, was born into. Instead of being killed, Moses (under the plan and protection of Almighty God) was adopted by Pharaoh's daughter. After 40 years of being brought up in the palace, Moses took it upon himself to correct what he saw as an injustice. He ended up killing an Egyptian and had to flee for his life.

Fleeing to the land of Midian, he settled down with a Midianite family, married, and spent the next 40 years taking care of his father-in-law's flocks. At the end of those forty years, he found out that God

did, indeed, have a plan for the descendants of Abraham and that he was to be involved in that plan.

GOD HAS NOT FORGOTTEN.

At a time of life when Moses might have been thinking of a nice, well-earned retirement, he discovered that his usefulness to God was just beginning. After getting Moses' attention through a burning bush that did not burn up, God revealed Himself to Moses as the God who can be trusted.

God's timing is perfect.

During the time the Israelites were in slavery they were unaware that God had told Abraham that there was a definite time limit to their slavery. When seen from their point of view, it looked like God had abandoned them. They had never seen the land of Canaan. They had lived in Egypt all their lives. They prayed but it looked like their prayers fell on deaf ears. Dreary day followed dreary day in an endless cycle and nothing ever changed.

Like the Israelites we, too, see things from our own point of view and get impatient and fretful. Yet the testimony of Scripture is that God's timing is perfect. Oh, that we could learn to trust Him and wait upon Him!

Exodus chapter 3 reveals that in spite of the passage of many years, God was about to fulfill His promise to Abraham. He was just waiting for the right time.

God's promises are trustworthy.

I grew up in a family which had a reputation for integrity. My brothers started a business with the help of a loan from one of their friends who was quite prosperous. After spending several years paying him back he told them that a lot of people had "borrowed" money from him but they were the only ones who had actually paid him back. He was surprised and pleased.

We live in a broken world. Promises are given glibly and lightly. Nobody thinks it's a big deal to break a promise. Perhaps we have become so used to lies that we have trouble believing the promises of God.

God's plan involves using people.

God could have delivered His people by doing it Himself, not involving Moses and Aaron at all. He could have sent angels to do the job. Instead, He chose to use fallible, faulty, feeble human beings to do the work He chose for them to do.

As we see God's interaction with various people in scripture, we become aware that God was the one who chose them. Joshua was chosen by God to succeed Moses. He was not chosen by the Israelites. Jeremiah, when he was called to be a prophet, objected that he was too young. God did not accept this excuse and informed him that He had commissioned him to be a prophet even before he was born. John the Baptist' life and ministry was foretold to his father before John was even born.

As God talked to Moses about what He was going to do for His people, Moses' heart must have rejoiced. His joy was soon replaced by dismay when God said, *"So now, go. I am sending you to Pharaoh to bring my people the Israelites out of Egypt."* Moses then spent time trying to convince God that he was the wrong man for the job. God, though, sees the future and knows Moses is just the right man.

It is the same today. Ephesians 2:8-10 make it clear that we are saved by grace instead of the works we do. Our salvation, however, results in good works which God has prepared in advance for us to do.

GOD DOES NOT LET SIN GO UNPUNISHED FOREVER.

God had set a time limit but His people were unaware of it. They had begun to think that misery and oppression was just a natural part of life. All of a sudden, Moses and Aaron entered the picture and brought the good news that God was about to change things. From

Exodus chapter 5 through chapter 12 we see God revealing Himself to the Egyptians.

God tried to get their attention by plagues.

God started out with a small request to Pharaoh. The request was for him to allow the Israelites to go on a three-day journey into the wilderness. This is something that Pharaoh could have granted easily enough. Instead, he refused and made impossible labor demands on them.

Moses and Aaron did a miracle in front of Pharaoh but he was unmoved. Shortly thereafter God showed His power by turning their water to blood – inconvenient but not life-threatening. God does not lower the boom all at once without any kind of a warning. He gives sinners a chance to repent.

Each plague was more serious than the previous one.

The next plague was the plague of frogs. They were a nuisance, as were the gnats and the flies. No one, though, has ever died from a swarm of gnats or flies.

The next plague was more serious. It caused the death of all the Egyptian livestock. God further showed His power by striking only the Egyptians. Not a single Israelite cow was affected.

The plague of boils was extremely painful, but the plague of hail was deadly to 1.) the servants that were in the field, 2.) the livestock, and 3.) the crops. As if that were not bad enough, then came the locusts and destroyed the part of the crop that was not destroyed by the hail.

The next plague was that of darkness. We sometimes get depressed on gray days. Think of the confusion and disorientation during the three days of total darkness.

The last plague ended in death.

There was one more plague to come – the death of the firstborn of everyone in Egypt. From a mere nuisance, to pain, economic devastation, and finally, death. The saddest part of this whole situation is that it could have been stopped at any time if Pharaoh would have humbled himself and given in to God's demands.

God gave plenty of warning and plenty of chances for repentance but all to no avail. Maybe a good lesson for our lives is: "If You feel like you are spinning your wheels, turn around and go the other direction and God might let go of the bumper!"

GOD'S DELIVERANCE WAS COMPLETE. GOD DOES NOT DO A HALFWAY JOB. EXODUS 14

While the Egyptians were mourning their loss, Pharaoh sent word to Moses to leave. God had accomplished His purpose, but He was not through yet.

The Bible says that God Himself led them by means of a cloud that turned to a pillar of fire at night. It is also recorded in Exodus 13:8 that God led them in a roundabout way.

He purposely led them to encamp by the Red Sea. Meanwhile the Egyptians were suddenly realizing that they had lost their labor force, and were going after them to try to bring them back.

Can you imagine the panic of God's people? "What do we do now? We can't get across this sea and the enemy is right behind us!" It is time for God to show His power. He parts the sea so they can go across on dry ground!

The enemy was completely destroyed.

The Egyptians were kept from attacking the Israelites by the cloud of God which had moved to the rear of the Israelite camp and gave brightness to God's people but darkness to God's enemies. After His people were safely across, God allowed the Egyptian army to plunge headlong into their own destruction. Exodus 14: 23-28 tells the story of their death. Verse 28 records the fact that not one of them survived.

God's people learned a lesson in faith.

After the third plague on the land of Egypt, God exempted His people from any further plagues. There were swarms of flies in Egypt but not one fly in the land of Goshen where the Israelites lived. Egyptian people had painful boils. Israelites had none. They must have rejoiced at these judgments and their faith must have grown as they realized their God was acting on their behalf.

At the parting of the sea, however, their faith must have been raised to a higher level. I often wonder how long it would take to forget a miracle that was so obviously the power of an almighty God who was worthy of their love and devotion.

God's name was glorified.

Chapter 15 of Exodus records the song of praise that the Israelites sang the next day. God's power and love were celebrated and there was singing and dancing.

Why is it such a big deal that God was glorified? It is simply that we, as human beings, are created with a need to worship. If we have no idea who God is, we will worship something, even if that something is our own self. Abraham's ancestors worshipped the moon. The nations in Caanan worshipped a god named Baal. They made statues and images of what they imagined he looked like. The men of Athens, in Paul's day, worshipped many gods. They even had a statue dedicated to "the unknown God."

Everything God did since the creation of the world had the purpose of revealing Himself to mankind, especially His work in bringing His people out of slavery. The Israelites needed to know God's power, God's love for them, and God's judgment on those who rebelled against Him. They needed to know these things so they could worship Him, "in spirit and in truth", as Jesus said, thousands of years later, to the woman at the well.

As we look back at the mighty power and the awesome plan of God, we need to realize that it was for OUR benefit that these things were written down. God has lost none of His power and God still loves unlovely people. MAY GOD BE GLORIFIED IN OUR LIFE!!!

God had accomplished one part of His plan. He had gotten his people out of Egypt. Now He began the process of getting Egypt out of His people.

Chapter 5

GOD INSTRUCTS HIS PEOPLE

Exodus 19:1 & 2 *"On the first day of the third month after the Israelites left Egypt – on that very day – they came to the Desert of Sinai. After they set out from Rephidim, they entered the Desert of Sinai, and Israel camped there in the desert in front of the mountain."*

God's people have now seen His power in delivering them from slavery. They have experienced His protection of them at the Red Sea. They have enjoyed the benefits of His provision for them as He provided water and food. Now He wants to move them to a higher level in their relationship by giving them guidelines for life.

A marriage is established by the taking and receiving of vows. The groom makes promises to the bride. She makes promises to him. Those vows strengthen the bond between them. Their love grows as they live out those promises in everyday life.

The ten commandments can be considered the wedding vows between God and Israel. Several times in the Bible God speaks of His relationship to Israel as a marriage relationship. God gave many more instructions to the people, but the ten commandments were the basic framework. God says, in effect, "If you love Me, I want to give you some laws that will benefit your relationship with Me and your relationship with each other." These laws can be broken down into three areas.

FOUR RULES TO GOVERN OUR RELATIONSHIP WITH GOD

The first four commandments have to do with how we relate to God. I have a pastor friend who often said, "If we could get the first four right, maybe we wouldn't have so much trouble with the other six."

Put Him first. Make Him our highest priority.

God is not just a Sunday God! He is not even a Sunday and Wednesday night God. He is either Lord of All of our lives or He is not Lord AT all. Jesus said, *"Why do you call me 'Lord, Lord' and do not do what I say?" Luke 6:46*

How can we put Him first in our everyday life? Does that mean we have to be on our knees in prayer for hours on end? Does that mean we have to have our noses stuck in the Bible for most of the day? No! It simply means loving what He loves and hating what He hates. It means adopting His values about what is important in life. It means letting Him transform us rather than conforming to the world's ideas and values.

"Do not conform to the pattern of this world but be transformed by the renewing of your mind. Then you will be able to test and approve what God's will is – His good, pleasing and perfect will." Romans 12:2

No idols. No image we make can capture God's glory.

People seem to have a natural desire to make statues and images of what they imagine their god to look like. They have a need to see what they worship. When the apostle Paul was in Athens he was "distressed to see that the city was full of idols." (Acts 17:6) Later when he got a chance to preach to them he declared, *"For as I walked around and looked carefully at your objects of worship, I even found an altar with this inscription: 'to an unknown God.' Now what you worship as something unknown I am going to proclaim to you." Acts 17:23)*

Idolatry was one of the sins the Israelites were addicted to until their captivity in Babylon. After they returned to the land from the Babylonian captivity, they never again worshipped idols.

Some of the idols they worshipped were beautiful, finely crafted works of art. Others were ugly, gruesome images that inspired fear. Whether they were beautiful or ugly, these idols had one thing in common – they were powerless, dead chunks of wood or metal.

Respect His name. Do not use it loosely.

This command did not mean the same for the people of that day that it might for us today. Basically, this command was to prevent the taking of vows or oaths in God's name when they didn't have any intention of keeping it.

For the most part, this command was obeyed. They had a great reverence for the holiness of God's name. The scribes, when they had to write the name of God, would take a quill that had never been used, then throw the quill away after they had written God's name. They would avoid saying God's name by substituting the word, "Lord".

It grieves me greatly that down through the years we have lost that reverence and awe. We have cheapened His name to the point where it is used as a curse instead of a blessing.

Respect His plan for weekly activities. Set the Sabbath day apart as holy.

Speaking of the seventh day, Genesis 2:3 says *"God blessed the seventh day and set it apart as special. It was, I believe, a perpetual reminder of the work God had done in six days."*

Did God rest on that day because He was completely exhausted from working so hard? No! He rested on that day because He had completed everything that need to be done. Work does not exhaust God because He is not subject to our limitations.

As well as having one day a week serve as a reminder of God's creative activity there is another reason. The God who created the human body knows what is best for that body. He knows that we need to work and He knows that we need to rest as well. If we work but don't rest, we burn out. If we rest but don't work, we rust out. In giving His rules and regulations to the Israelites, God made sure that on special occasions (like feast days) no work was to be done.

Since the 7th day of the week was Saturday, not Sunday, why don't we go to church on Saturday? Some people do, but early Christians got into the habit of gathering on Sunday to celebrate the day the Lord rose from the dead.

A BRIDGE BETWEEN OUR RELATIONSHIP TO OTHER PEOPLE – FAMILY RELATIONSHIPS

Family is important to God. He has designed the family to be the biggest blessing in our lives. Unfortunately, it can also be the biggest heartache when those relationships go sour because of sin.

Our family relationships are a pattern for our relationship with others.

I was taught at a very early age the value of respect. Respect for my parents branched out to respect for all other adults, especially those in authority. Not only did my parents insist on it – they modeled it. They showed respect for each other, their neighbors and their friends.

In the same way I developed a work ethic that was passed on to them by THEIR parents. I never knew either of my grandfathers but I know how they felt about hard work. As a result, during my adult years I usually worked at least two jobs for fear of being thought lazy.

If a child learns to be obedient to a parent, they will find it easier to be obedient to a teacher or to a boss.

It is the first command that had a promise attached to it.

The command is "Honor your father and mother, so that you may live long in the land the Lord your God is giving you."

Surely, that is not taken to mean that every single individual that honors their parents is going to live a long and happy life. There are many people who have kept this command and yet died at an early age. So how, then, should we interpret the promise?

I believe that we should keep in mind the people to whom God was speaking. God wanted to pour blessing after blessing on the nation of Israel. He wanted to give them a land they could enjoy, but it was conditional on their obedience. If they learned obedience and respect from their parents, chances are, they would be obedient and respectful to others and to God Himself. If they would do that, they would have a better chance at a good long life.

This is a principle that carries over into our lives today. If we learn the lessons God wants us to learn from our families, we have a better chance at living a life that God can bless.

The penalty for continual defiance of parents was death.

There were some sins in God's law that were serious enough to be punishable by death. One of these sins was **continual** defiance of parental authority.

In Deuteronomy 21:18-21 it states, *"If someone has a stubborn and rebellious son who does not obey his father and mother and will not listen to them when they discipline him, his father and mother shall take hold of him and bring him to the elders at the gate of the town. They shall say to the elders, 'This son of ours is stubborn and rebellious. He will not obey us. He is a glutton and a drunkard.' Then all the men of his town are to stone him to death. You must purge the evil from among you. All Israel will hear of it and be afraid.*

This extreme measure is to be the last resort, but if all else fails then death is the result. I conclude from this that God is serious about honoring parents!

HOW TO RELATE TO OTHER PEOPLE

The next five commands are short and to the point. They can basically be summed up by the word, "respect".

No murder: respect for life created in God's image.

Long before the ten commandments were given, God had told Noah that murder was punishable by death. Genesis 9:6 says, *"Whoever sheds human blood, by humans shall their blood be shed; for in the image of God has God made mankind."*

No adultery: respect for the vows of marriage.

When God created the first man and woman, He performed the first marriage ceremony. This is what Jesus referred to when the Pharisees asked Him about whether divorce was legal. No matter how we have justified and rationalized immoral behavior, God has not changed His mind. His ideal is one man and one woman until death parts them. He has designed us as sexual beings, but only within the bounds of marriage.

No theft: respect for other's possessions.

We had locks on our doors in the house where I grew up, but we seldom used them. The only time I can remember my folks locking the doors was when we went on vacation. My, how times have changed! I have to admit that I have given in to the mistrust that grips our society. I have gotten into the habit of locking my car and have purchased a security system for my home.

No lying: respect for integrity.

In 1993 the Port Authority of New York and New Jersey ran a help-wanted ad. The ad asked for engineers who had expertise in using Sontag connectors. The ad yielded 170 responses. The problem? There is no such thing as a Sontag connector. The ad was written just to see how many people falsify their resume.

We don't even call it lying anymore. We say, "I mis-spoke." We call it strategic misrepresentation. We call it "reality augmentation."

It is bad enough when we lie to others but the first chapter of the book of James says we can lie to ourselves. We can tell ourselves that God is not as good to us as He should be. We can tell ourselves that obedience is optional. Finally, we can kid ourselves into thinking that it doesn't matter what we say.

No coveting: respect for the success of others.

What is coveting, anyway? It is an intense desire for something which someone else has. This not only relates to possessions – it can also relate to an ability or talent they have.

Chapter 6

GOD DWELLS AMONG HIS PEOPLE

Exodus 25:1 & 2: " The Lord said to Moses, 'Tell the Israelites to bring me an offering. You are to receive the offering for me from everyone whose heart prompts them to give.' "

Exodus 25:8 & 9: "Then have them make a sanctuary for me, and I will dwell among them. Make this tabernacle and all its furnishings exactly like the pattern I will show you."

FOLLOW GOD'S PLAN. Exodus 26:30-33

Moses was told many times to follow God's instructions to the letter in building the tabernacle. Nothing was left to the imagination of human beings. God knew exactly what He wanted done and communicated it clearly.

One great achievement of my father's life was the construction of a log house. He didn't pay someone to build it because he had in his mind exactly what he wanted it to look like. He put every log in place by himself. I was privileged to help with some of the final details but I did not contribute any new ideas. All I did was to follow his instructions.

God not only knew what it was to look like, He knew the construction materials and even who would be the main workers.

The marvelous thing about this building project is that the Israelites had everything they needed to construct it. They didn't have to have a fund-raising drive or a bake sale or garage sale.

Another thing about the tabernacle, it was portable. It could be taken down and set up in a very short time. In other words, it was a perfect dwelling place for a God who wanted to be involved in the travels of His people.

Exodus 26:30-36 gives instructions for separating the Most Holy Place from the Holy Place. It talks about the table for the bread and the placement of the lampstand and the altar of incense. Then it speaks of the curtain for the entrance to the tent. Later instructions talk about the altar of burnt offering and the courtyard around the tabernacle.

The Bible is filled with many examples of people who heard instructions from God and deviated from those instructions. In 100% of those cases, it ended in disaster. The construction of the tabernacle was not one of those cases. Everything was done according to God's plan.

ACKNOWLEDGE GOD'S PRESENCE. Exodus 29:42-46

Exodus 29:42-46 "For the generations to come this burnt offering is to be made regularly at the entrance to the tent of meeting before the Lord. There I will meet you and speak to you; there also I will consecrate the tent of meeting and the altar and will consecrate Aaron and his sons to serve me as priests. Then I will dwell among the Israelites and be their God. They will know that I am the Lord their God who brought them out of Egypt so that I might dwell among them. I am the Lord their God."

We know God is present when His workers are willing.

God had two main workers that He wanted to use to build the tabernacle but there were many others as well. The two primary workers were Bezalel from the tribe of Judah, and Oholiab from the tribe of Dan.

The Bible says in Exodus 35:30-35 that the Lord had filled these two men with wisdom to know how to make the designs that the Lord wanted them to make.

Not only had He given these two men the wisdom necessary to do His work, He also gave them the ability to teach others.

This is a principle we find throughout scripture. We are not only to do the work God has called us to do. We are to pass it on to others. That is why Jesus called us to go and make disciples. I thank God every day for the godly men He has put in my life. They have taken the time to teach me what they know.

We know God is present when the work is completed according to God's satisfaction.

Chapters 36 through 39 of Exodus tell in detail the construction of the tabernacle and the materials used. All the work is summed up in these words: *Exodus 39:32 "So all the work on the tabernacle, the tent of meeting, was completed. The Israelites did everything just as the Lord commanded Moses."*

How do we know that God is present in our efforts for Him? It is when our motives are right, our methods are right, and our message glorifies and exalts the Lord instead of ourselves.

There were no mistakes in the building of the Lord's house. God was the overseer of everything that was done. They could confidently present it to Moses, knowing that he would find it up to standard.

EXPERIENCE GOD'S GLORY. Exodus 40:34-38

Exodus chapter 40 tells the story of Moses setting up the tabernacle after everything had been made.

When Moses finished this work, the glory of the Lord filled the tabernacle. Moses could not enter it because the glory of the Lord was so great.

After that time the presence of the Lord was associated with His dwelling place. When the cloud lifted from the tabernacle the Israelites would set out on the march. Chapter 40:38 says, *"So the cloud of the Lord was over the tabernacle by day, and fire was in the cloud by night, in the sight of all the Israelites during all their travels."*

Do you ever wish that the Lord would show Himself to us in such a visible way? Don't you wish God would leave you a note on the kitchen table? Perhaps you think if you saw a such a sign your faith would be stronger. I think not! God has given us today more than a visible sign. He has given us His Holy Spirit that helps us to understand His word, helps us to pray, and gives us power to repent of sin and get the victory over it.

Chapter 7

REFUSING GOD'S BLESSINGS

Numbers 14:1-4 "Then all the congregation raised a loud cry, and the people wept that night. And all the people of Israel grumbled against Moses and Aaron. The whole congregation said to them, 'Would that we had died in the land of Egypt! Or would that we had died in this wilderness! Why is the Lord bringing us into this land, to fall by the sword? Our wives and our little ones will become a prey. Would it not be better for us to go back to Egypt?' And they said to one another, 'Let us choose a leader and go back to Egypt.'"

"The sky is falling! The sky is falling! I must go to London to tell the king!" This is the first line of an old story. The main character, Chicken Little, is hit on the head by an acorn so she concludes that the sky must be falling.

She starts on her way to tell the king and is joined by several feathered friends. Finally, they are joined by Foxy-loxy who ends up eating every one of them.

Alas! Nobody got to London to tell the king the sky was falling. It didn't matter, however, because the sky wasn't falling anyway.

This silly story illustrates a valuable principle of life. Our circumstances in life can often cause us to make faulty decisions based on false assumptions. This is called "panic." This what God's people were guilty of.

Panic occurs in our life when we make decisions based on false assumptions.

God's intention was to give His people the land of Canaan as a permanent dwelling place. If they would follow His leading, He would enable them to conquer the land. Instead of following His leading, the people were filled with fear and rejected God's plan for them.

THEY ASSUMED THAT GOD HAD GIVEN THEM AN IMPOSSIBLE JOB.

See Numbers 13:26-33. Fear is the opposite of faith. Fear paralyzes us and causes us to act in ways that are irrational. Fear looks at the size of the giants – faith looks at the size of God.

There were twelve spies that went into the promised land. Ten were filled with fear and two were filled with faith.

The two tried to encourage the congregation by pointing out that God was bigger than any giant. They were unsuccessful in their efforts. It is just as if the crowd had said, "We've made up our minds. Don't confuse us with the facts."

There are numerous examples in scripture of God giving victory against overwhelming odds. Gideon, just one example, did not have a great deal of faith but ended up following God's leading. He (and God) defeated a vast horde of Midianites with 300 men.

God had shown His power and His provision for the people ever since they left Egypt. Their fear caused them to forget these things and to concentrate on the problem.

How many times in our own life are we confronted with a problem that seems insurmountable and causes us to lose hope instead of seek help?

THEY ASSUMED THAT GOD DIDN'T REALLY LOVE THEM.

After hearing about giants in the land, they spent the night weeping and grumbling and plotting a rebellion. These people had been praying for years for an end to their slavery. Now they wanted to go back there? Go figure!

Sometimes our selfishness causes us to question God's love. We define His love as one that exempts us from all problems in life. "Why am I sick? God must not love me." "Why didn't I get that job I wanted? God must not love me."

Many years later, after their return from the Babylonian captivity the Israelites were openly questioning God's love. See Malachi 1:2

THEY ASSUMED THAT GOD DIDN'T REALLY MEAN WHAT HE SAID.

As we go through Numbers 14, we see the faithlessness of the people but we also see the grief and distress of the people of faith.

Moses and Aaron fell facedown before the Lord. Joshua and Caleb tore their clothes, (a sign of grief and distress) and tried to reason with the crowd.

Finally, the glory of the Lord appeared to them and the Lord pronounced judgment on them. The judgment was this: they would wander in the wilderness for 40 years until that whole generation over 20 years old had died. They would not get to possess the land, but their children would. The only two exceptions to this rule were Joshua and Caleb.

The ten spies who had spread the bad report about the land were struck down and died at that very time.

Let us review. The Israelites saw the glory of God as He came to their camp. They experienced His anger as He pronounced sentence upon them. They witnessed the sudden death of the ten spies. Could there be any doubt at all in their minds that God meant what He said? We would think that there was no way they would fail to take God seriously. Incredibly, though, that was not the case.

The next morning, they offered a lame acknowledgment of their sin and set out to fight the enemy. Moses warned them not to do it because the Lord was not with them. What was the result of their feeble efforts?

Numbers 14:44 & 45 says, "Nevertheless, in their presumption, they went up toward the highest point in the hill country, though neither Moses nor the ark of the Lord's covenant moved from the camp. Then the Amalekites and the Canaanites who lived in that hill country came down and attacked them and beat them down all the way to Hormah."

What lesson for our lives can we take from this example of failure? What are the giants in your life? Have you let fear get the upper hand over faith? God does not force you to take the blessings that He wants to pour out on your life. He leaves that up to you. Remember, however, that the result of rejecting God's blessings is a wasted life. You will end up wandering around in the desert and never get into the promised land.

The good news, however, is that failure is not final. God's plan cannot be thwarted. It was ultimately fulfilled for the next generation.

Chapter 8

RECEIVING GOD'S BLESSINGS

Joshua 1:1 & 2 After the death of Moses the servant of the Lord, the Lord said to Joshua the son of Nun, Moses' assistant, "Moses my servant is dead. Now therefore arise, go over the Jordan, you and all this people, into the land that I am giving to them, to the people of Israel.

Joshua 1:8 This book of the law shall not depart from your mouth, but you shall meditate on it day and night, so that you may be careful to do according to all that is written in it. For then you will make your way prosperous, and then you will have good success.

One thing God had made very clear to Abraham was that He would give his descendants a land of their own. It was the very land that Abraham was living in as an alien and a stranger. The only part of the land which Abraham owned was a burial place.

We saw in the last chapter that, because of unbelief, the Israelites ended up wandering around in the desert for forty years instead of conquering the land God wanted to give them. Now a new generation has arisen and God's promises are fulfilled. The book of Joshua is a record of what happens when you obey God.

A NEW LEADER IS CHOSEN.

God's servant, Moses, was dead but God's plan and purpose was not altered. He chose someone who was able to complete what Moses had begun. There were several things that were significant about this leader and his encounter with the God of the universe.

The new leader was chosen by God and not by the people.

God's people did not have a very good track record of choosing leaders.

While Moses was up on the mountain talking to God, the people turned to Aaron and wanted him to make a god for them that they

could see. What they wanted in a leader was someone who followed all their wishes.

Later they wanted to choose a leader and go back to Egypt instead of doing the job God wanted them to do.

Who would you choose for a leader if it were up to you? Would you choose John Wayne or Don Knotts – aka Barney Fife? We show our preferences in many instances by whom we call for a pastor. We want someone who is 35 years old and has 40 years of experience. We want someone who condemns sin but never hurts anyone's feelings. We want someone who is always serious, but has a great sense of humor!

It is important to me that it was God who called Joshua because unless it is God that calls you to a task, you are laboring in vain. Has God called you to be pastor of XYZ church, or have you been chosen by the church members because you had a great resume?

God is the one who knows us thoroughly. Therefore, He is the one who is qualified to choose. Psalm 139 talks about God's knowledge. He not only knows our words and our thoughts - He knows what we will or will not accomplish. Verse 16 says, "*Your eyes saw my unformed substance; in Your book were written, every one of them, the days that were formed for me, when as yet there was none of them.*"

A promise is given.

Do you remember the day you started a new job? Maybe your heart rate was up, your palms were sweaty and your mind was filled with anxiety. Imagine what a comfort it would have been to you if, at that moment, you heard the voice of God saying to you, "You will succeed in this job. You will not only succeed, but you will excel."

Imagine how Joshua must have felt when he found out he was God's choice to be the new leader of the people. He must have felt inadequate to fill Moses' big sandals. God knew how he felt. Therefore, this promise was given to strengthen and encourage him.

God, who knows us thoroughly, also knows how to give us a promise when we need it. Sometimes He speaks through His Word, sometimes He speaks through other believers and sometimes He speaks to us directly.

He spoke to Paul with a word of comfort. Acts 18:9 says *"And the Lord said to Paul one night in a vision, 'Do not be afraid, but go on speaking and do not be silent, for I am with you and no one will attack you to harm you, for I have many in this city who are my people.'"*

He spoke to Peter with a word of guidance. After Peter's vision of the sheet let down from heaven, he found that three men were looking for him. (These were the ones that Cornelius had sent to him.) Acts 10:19 & 20 says, *"And while Peter was pondering this vision, the Spirit said to him, 'Behold, three men are looking for you. Rise and go down and accompany them without hesitation, for I have sent them.'"*

You may be asking, "Why doesn't God ever speak to me directly like He spoke to Paul and to Peter?" One possibility is that the early days of Christianity was a time of transition. Since those days, we have the complete Bible to read. We didn't get to see Jesus' miracles, but we can read about them and believe. We didn't get to hear Jesus teach, but we can read His words and have faith. Thomas believed because he had the evidence right before his eyes, but Jesus said, "Blessed are those that to do not see and yet believe."

Another possibility is that God will speak to you directly when He feels it is necessary. In my 50+ years of being a Christian, God has spoken to me twice. One was a word of comfort and one was a word of rebuke. It was something that was badly needed at the time. There were two things that made those experiences remarkable. 1.) I had no doubt that it was God speaking. 2.) It was an unforgettable experience.

A command is given

God's word to Joshua about being strong and courageous is not just good advice. It is a command. Joshua 1:9 says, *"Have I not commanded you? Be strong and courageous. Do not be frightened, and do not be dismayed, for the Lord your God is with you wherever you go."*

God commands courage, then gives a reason for that courage. The reason that Joshua can be encouraged is the promise that God made to be with him wherever he went. It is not just a blind optimism. It is based squarely on the word of the Lord.

Down through the ages God's faithful servants have become discouraged, depressed and despairing. In all of those cases God spoke into those situations and gave them new hope. Just a quick reading of the Psalms tells us that in spite of our circumstances, God is bigger than the situation we face.

Psalm 73 was written by Israel's chief minister of music. Asaph gives a testimony of his conflict. He is filled with dismay over the unrighteousness of people and wonders why God doesn't seem to be doing anything about it. The turning point in his attitude appears in verse 17. When he sees things from God's point of view, he gains new understanding. He realizes that God will punish sin in His time and not our time.

The Old Testament prophet, Habakkuk, had the same problem as the psalmist. He questions God about His dealings with the unrighteous and waits upon God to give him an answer. When God gives him the answer, Habakkuk was satisfied. His new attitude is summed up in the closing verses of chapter 3. Hab. 3:17-19 says, *"Though the fig tree should not blossom, nor fruit be on the vines, the produce of the olive fail and the fields yield no food, the flock be cut off from the fold and there be no herd in the stalls, Yet I will rejoice in the Lord; I will take joy in the God of my salvation. God, the Lord, is my strength; he makes my feet like the deer's; he makes me tread on my high places."*

Even John the Baptist had a season of doubt. He was faithful in all that the Lord had given him to do, yet here he was, locked up in prison. It was unfair! Why didn't Jesus come and get him out? He sent two disciples to ask Jesus, "Are you the one who should come or should we expect another?" Jesus' answer to him was that the works He was doing spoke for themselves. Jesus didn't do miracles to show off but to show that He was from God.

The lesson we can learn from this is that God is still God, even when He doesn't do what we think He should do or act when we think He should act. If we base our hope on God's promises and let ourselves be comforted by God's encouragement we will not be overwhelmed by the storms of life.

A warning is given.

Joshua 1:7 "Only be very strong and very courageous, being careful to do according to all the law that Moses my servant commanded you. Do not turn from it to the right hand or to the left, that you may have good success wherever you go." In other words, obedience to God is not optional. If you deviate from it you are asking for trouble. Be careful to do what God says. Do only what God says and do all that God says.

The book of Hebrews talks about Moses and commends him as a faithful servant of God. He was, indeed, faithful but Numbers 20:2-12 tell the story of how Moses deviated from what God told him to do.

The Israelites quarreled with Moses (and God) because they were out of water. Moses and Aaron prayed to God and God answered them immediately. Numbers 20:8 has the Lord saying to Moses, *"Take the staff and assemble the congregation, you and Aaron your brother, and tell the rock before their eyes to yield its water. So you will bring water out of the rock for them and give drink to the congregation and their cattle."*

Consider this: Moses prayed, God answered him and told him specifically what to do. Why did Moses not follow the instruction? He took his staff; he and the elders went to the rock but instead of speaking to it he struck it with his staff.

God, in his mercy, provided water for the people but was displeased with the disobedience of Moses. It was because of this one thing that Moses was kept from bringing the Israelites into the promised land.

We see later on in the history of the nation that the first king of Israel did **almost** what God wanted him to do but not all. King Saul was told to destroy all the people and all the livestock of a people known as the Amalekites – ancient enemies of God and God's people. Saul just couldn't bring himself to destroy all that fine livestock. Another act of disobedience was in keeping the king of the Amalekites alive instead of killing him.

As in the case of Moses, this act of partial obedience was costly to him. It cost him God's favor. From that time on he became jealous, irrational and paranoid.

A NEW LAND IS CONQUERED.

Genesis chapter 12 records the story of Abraham (at the age of 75) leaving the city of Haran and going to the land of Canaan in obedience to the Lord's command. He arrives in the land and travels through it as God leads him. Genesis 12:7 is the first of many promises to Abraham that God was going to give this land to his descendants.

Genesis 15 talks about another promise to Abraham about the land. At that time God made clear to him that the inheritance of the land would not be for many years.

God renewed the promise to Abraham's son Isaac and then to Isaac's son Jacob. Jacob's son, Joseph, also believed strongly in God's promise. He made his relatives swear that they would take his bones with them to the land of Canaan when the Lord delivered them out of Egypt.

Here, at the beginning of the book of Joshua, we have the promise about to be fulfilled. Centuries have gone by, yet God is not slow concerning His promises. He is always just in time.

How to cross a river without getting wet – obey God.

Before God's people could enter the land, they had to cross the Jordan river. How could such a great horde of people get across the river? Could they wade? Could they swim? Could they build a bridge? The Jordan river was, indeed, shallow in some places but at this time of year it was at flood stage. God gave them instructions to follow.

Joshua 3:14-17 says, "So when the people set out from their tents to pass over the Jordan with the priests bearing the ark of the covenant before the people, and as soon as those bearing the ark had come as far as the Jordan, and the feet of the priests bearing the ark were dipped in the brink of the water (now the Jordan overflows all its banks throughout the time of harvest), the waters coming down from above stood and rose up in a heap very far away, at Adam, the city that is beside Zarethan, and those flowing down toward the Sea of the Arabah, the Salt Sea, were completely cut off. And the people passed over opposite Jericho. Now the priests bearing the ark of the covenant of the Lord stood firmly on dry ground in the midst of the Jordan, and all Israel was passing over on dry ground until all the nation finished passing over the Jordan."

What an unusual way to get across a river! Nobody even got their feet wet. They didn't have to dig out their swimsuits. They didn't have to find their snorkels. All they had to do was obey God.

This was only the beginning of many ways that God was going to display His power over the forces of nature and power over His enemies.

How to defeat an enemy that is stronger than you – obey God.

Now that they were in the land, they had the job of conquering it. There is a lesson here for us. God gave the land, but they must possess it. So, also, God gives us gifts but we need to make use of them. The Bible admonishes us to "work out our salvation with fear and trembling." This means we are to take what God has given us and use it to good advantage so others will be attracted to the gracious God we serve. See Matthew 5:16.

The first city they had to conquer was the city of Jericho. There were basically two ways of conquering a walled city. 1.) Your army could surround the city so nobody could go in or come out. Eventually they would starve to death (or run out of toilet paper). 2.) You could batter down their walls with a battering ram.

One day while Joshua was out in the field by himself, the commander of the army of the Lord (aka Jesus) introduced Himself to Joshua and gave him the battle plan. Joshua 6:2-5 lets us in on the plan. *"And the Lord said to Joshua, 'See, I have given Jericho into your hand, with its king and mighty men of valor. You shall march around the city, all the men of war going around the city once. Thus shall you do for six days. Seven priests shall bear seven trumpets of ram's horns before the ark. On the seventh day you shall march around the city seven times, and the priests shall blow the trumpets. And when they make a long blast with the ram's horn, when you hear the sound of the trumpet, then all the people shall shout with a great shout, and the wall of the city will fall down flat, and the people shall go up, everyone straight before him."*

What kind of crazy way was that to fight a war? The amazing thing about this unique battle plan is that everyone did exactly as they were told to do. Could it possibly be that God wanted to do it that way to see if they would obey Him? They didn't have to besiege the city. They didn't have to break down the walls. All they had to do was obey God.

How to defeat an enemy that should be easy to conquer – obey God.

Joshua 7:1 "But the people of Israel broke faith in regard to the devoted things, for Achan the son of Carmi, son of Zabdi, son of Zerah, of the tribe of Judah, took some of the devoted things. And the anger of the Lord burned against the people of Israel."

After the mighty victory at Jericho the people were probably feeling like they were on a roll and nothing could stand in their way. Joshua sent two spies to the next city on their agenda. They came back all full of confidence and said, in effect, "No problem! That city is a tiny one compared to Jericho. We should be able to conquer it with three thousand soldiers. Easy-peasy! Piece of cake!"

Joshua sent the men to the city of Ai and, much to their dismay, they had no power over the enemy at all. In fact, thirty-six Israelite soldiers were killed. This was not supposed to happen. Did God not promise them victory over their enemies?

Instead of making a new battle plan or giving his troops a pep talk, Joshua and the elders did the right thing. They humbled themselves and fell on their faces before God.

In answer to their humble prayer, God answered them directly. Joshua 7:10-12 says, *"The Lord said to Joshua, 'Get up! Why have you fallen on your face? Israel has sinned; they have transgressed my covenant that I commanded them; they have taken some of the devoted things; they have stolen and lied and put them among their own belongings. Therefore, the people of Israel cannot stand before their enemies. They turn their backs before their enemies, because they have become devoted for destruction. I will be with you no more, unless you destroy the devoted things from among you.' "*

What, exactly, is a devoted thing? It is something that is set aside for a specific purpose. In this case it is something that belongs to the Lord. None of the people were to take anything from Jericho. The silver and gold were to be put into the treasury of the Lord and the rest of the things were to be burned.

The reader of this story already knows who committed the sin. But how is Joshua to find out? God prescribed a process by which His will was made known. Each tribe was to present itself before the Lord and He would indicate which tribe was to be chosen. After the tribe was chosen, each clan from the tribe presented itself. From the clans, each man was presented until they came to Achan.

Achan had no choice but to confess, after seeing that his hand was caught in the cookie jar. He is like so many of us today that have learned lessons from observing our dogs. "Always admit your sin (after you have been dragged out from under the bed.")

Why was God so mad? Why hold it against the whole nation because one man sinned? Achan was a part of a community that had a covenant relationship with the God of the universe. As a member of that community, he had an obligation to live up to the conditions of that covenant. That was the reason the apostle Paul was so upset with the Corinthian church. One member was having an affair with his stepmother and they were treating it as no big deal. One bad apple spoils the whole barrel.

The only way the people could regain the favor of God was to carry out God's sentence of punishment. They took Achan and his family and stoned them to death, as God had directed. God's favor was restored and they won their next battle. I have met many people who have felt that their sin hurt only themselves, but that is not true.

A NEW LOVE FOR GOD IS ENCOURAGED.

When we read the book of Joshua, we might get the impression that the conquering of the land took place very quickly. Such is not the case. We find that Caleb was 85 years old when he claimed his inheritance. That indicates that they had been in the land for at least five years.

Although God had given victory after victory under the leadership of Joshua, there were still many enemies in the land. Judah failed to conquer Jerusalem. The tribe of Ephraim failed to drive out the Canaanites who lived in one of their towns. The tribe of Manasseh could not drive the Canaanites out of three of their cities. In spite of these failures, most of their major enemies had been defeated, so it can honestly be said that God had fulfilled His promise.

Toward the end of his life, Joshua called the leaders and elders of Israel together on at least two occasions. In Joshua chapter 23 we see that he gives a warning to be faithful to God if they want to continue to receive His blessings. In Joshua chapter 24 we see that Joshua calls them together again and issues a challenge.

Joshua reminded the people of God's faithfulness.

Joshua, speaking as if God Himself were speaking, reminds the people how deeply God was involved in their lives. What was it that God had done for them?

1.) God had called Abraham from a background of idol worship and called him to follow Him.
2.) He led Abraham to the land of Canaan.

3.) He gave him many descendants, through his son, Isaac, and his grandson, Jacob.

4.) He encouraged Jacob to go to Egypt to dwell. (It was, at first, a place of safety and only later became a place of slavery.)

5.) He raised up Moses and Aaron to deliver them from Egypt.

6.) He gave them victory in the land that He had promised them.

Joshua challenged the people to remain faithful to God and to serve Him only.

One of the reasons that God told them to destroy their enemies was that He knew the Israelites would be curious about the various gods the people of the land worshipped. The Canaanites not only made carved images and graven images but their worship involved sexual immorality and child sacrifice.

Apparently, in spite of all that God had done for them, there was a problem with idolatry. Perhaps they didn't actually bow down to a graven or carved image, but they were not totally faithful to God.

Unfortunately, there is a great tendency in all of us to give in to idolatry. An idol is anything that takes the place of God in our life. An idol is what shapes our life. At one period of my life, I professed to love God with all my heart. At the same time, I let my desires and addictions take the high ground.

Joshua challenged the people to love and serve God totally and they responded eagerly that they would do just that. He must have known that it was a purely emotional response instead of a whole-hearted commitment. He emphasized the seriousness of it and showed by example his desire to serve the Lord. Joshua 24:15 has become a well-known verse that is exhibited in many Christian homes today. *"…But as for me and my house, we will serve the Lord."*

Joshua made a covenant with the people to remind them of what they promised.

Joshua 24:25-27 "So Joshua made a covenant with the people that day, and put in place statutes and rules for them at Shechem. And Joshua wrote these words in the Book of the Law of God. And he took a large stone and set it up there under the terebinth that was by the sanctuary of the Lord. And Joshua said to all the people, 'Behold, this stone shall be a witness against us, for it has heard all the words of the Lord that He spoke to us. Therefore, it shall be a witness against you, lest you deal falsely with your God.' "

It was not unusual to set up a stone or a heap of stones as a memorial. This is the seventh one mentioned in the book of Joshua.

1.) Twelve stones at the crossing of the Jordan.
2.) A heap of stones over Achan to remind people of the consequences of sin.
3. A heap of stones over the king of Ai, which spoke of the restoration of God's favor.
4.) Plastered stones with God's law written on them.
5.) A heap of stones over the Amorite kings at Gibeon.
6.) An altar built by the trans-Jordan tribes as a witness that they, too, belonged to the nation of Israel.
7.) The stone at Shechem to remind the people of their covenant with the Lord.

Do we have anything that reminds us of our covenants? How about a wedding ring? How about a family heirloom? How about a photo album? More importantly, how about our Bible?

Chapter 9

GOD GIVES HIS PEOPLE A KING

Deuteronomy 17:14 & 15: "When you come to the land that the Lord your God is giving you, and you possess it and dwell in it and then say, 'I will set a king over me, like all the nations that are around me,' you may indeed set a king over you whom the Lord your God will choose. One from among your brothers you shall set as king over you. You may not put a foreigner over you, who is not your brother."

Psalm 78:70 & 71: He chose David His servant and took him from the sheepfolds; from following the nursing ewes He brought him to shepherd Jacob His people, Israel His inheritance.

As the book of Joshua is the high point in the life of the Israelites, so the book of Judges is the low point. They were mostly faithful to God as long as Joshua was alive. When Joshua died, so did their obedience to God.

In the book of Judges, it is written three times: "In those days there was no king in Israel." Judges 17:6 adds the words, "Everyone did what was right in his own eyes." The book is filled with the repeated cycle of disobedience, repentance, prayer and God's deliverance. God would raise up a military leader who would deliver them from their enemy. The renewed commitment to God, however, did not last long.

Fast forward 400 and some years. We find things a mess, spiritually. The high priest is old and blind. His sons are corrupt. God pronounces that there is judgment to come. At the same time, God is preparing a man who will be a true priest and judge to Israel – the man, Samuel.

Samuel was trained by Eli from a very young age. He grew up knowing and obeying God and became not only a priest to Israel, but a true judge. The people were content to have him as a leader until he grew old and his sons did not have the integrity that he did. That's when the people asked God for a king.

God had already looked forward to this time. The verse at the beginning of this chapter was spoken by Moses even before they went into the land of Canaan. It describes who the king should be, what he should do, and what he should not do.

He was to be one of their own. He was to write for himself a copy of God's law and read it regularly. He was not supposed to make trade deals with Egypt, was not to acquire many wives and was not to acquire a great deal of wealth.

God gave the people what they asked for, even if it wasn't the best thing for them. The first king started out well but ended very badly. So, this time God chose another king – the man, David. He was Israel's greatest king.

GOD CHOSE DAVID WHILE HE WAS STILL A YOUNG SHEPHERD BOY.

Samuel was broken-hearted over how Saul had turned away from following God's ways. Chapter 16 of the book of 1st Samuel tells the story of Samuel doing his part in carrying out God's new plan.

God sent Samuel to the town of Bethlehem, to the house of a man named Jesse. He was to invite Jesse and his sons to a sacrifice and feast. God told him to anoint as king the one He chose. There are several things that stand out about God's choice of David.

He chose him over his older brothers.

It was customary in that time for the oldest son in a family to receive a double share of the estate. Along with the double share, he had more responsibility. He was to be the spiritual head of the household in place of the father.

There is just something special about the first-born. Parents take 5,000 pictures of them. The second-born rates only 2,000. By the time the third one comes along, the parents are still taking pictures – at least a dozen! (You would never guess that I am the youngest of three, would you?)

As Jesse and his family appeared at the sacrifice, Samuel asked Jesse's sons to appear before him, one by one. Keep in mind – at this point, Samuel had no idea who God's choice was. All he knew is that it was one of the sons, and that God would let him know.

As the oldest son appeared and strutted his stuff, Samuel was impressed. He was young, handsome and well-built. Surely, the Lord could use someone like that. To his surprise, he felt the Lord say to him, "Nope. That's not the one." As all seven sons passed before him, he heard the same answer from the Lord.

Finally, he asked Jesse if he had any more sons. Jesse admitted he had one more – the youngest, who was tending the family's sheep. He was sent for and the Lord said to Samuel, *"Arise, anoint him, for this is he."*

He chose him in spite of his humble job.

Shepherds were not looked upon with a great deal of respect at that time. If a family had sheep, the job of tending the flock was usually passed down to the youngest child.

Shepherds were looked upon with suspicion and disdain. Everyone knew that they were necessary but very few would deliberately pick the job of shepherd for a livelihood.

God Himself, however, thought it to be an honorable and important job. He called Abraham, Isaac and Jacob, who were all shepherds. And then he called Moses, who had spent forty years looking after his father-in-law's flock. God dignified the profession of shepherding by sending a group of angels to announce the birth of His son to shepherds. He didn't send the angels to the palace or the temple. He sent them to the field where the shepherds were.

Jesus, Himself, glorified the position of shepherd by announcing that He was the good shepherd. In one of the last conversations He had with Peter was an instruction to "feed His sheep."

Jesus made a distinction between Himself and other shepherds by the way they face danger. The shepherd who is just doing the job and not putting his heart into it will not face up to danger. Jesus, on the other hand, will go all the way for the good of the sheep – even unto death.

Psalm 23 pictures God as the perfect shepherd. He cares for our physical needs. He leads us to green pastures and still waters. He cares for our spiritual needs. He restores our soul and leads us in righteousness. He cares for our emotional needs. He gives us strength and comfort even in times of emotional turmoil. He provides for us, even in the face of our enemies. He leads us by blessing us in this life and giving us a sure hope for eternal life after death.

There are a lot of jobs in this world that people look down on, but God is not a snob. He was proud to call a lowly shepherd to be the king over His people.

He chose him for what was in his heart.

How easy it is for us to be deceived by appearances! 1st Samuel 16:6 shows that even godly Samuel was fooled by an impressive-looking young man. Samuel had invited Jesse and his sons to the sacrifice. 1st Samuel 16:6 says, *"When they came, he looked on Eliab and thought, 'Surely the Lord's anointed is before Him.' "* The next verse records God's response to him. 1st Samuel 16:7 says, *"But the Lord said to Samuel, 'Do not look upon his appearance or on the height of his stature, because I have rejected him. For the Lord sees not as man sees; man looks on the outward appearance, but the Lord looks on the heart.' "*

When Jesus started His ministry on this earth, He also chose men by what was in their heart. You would think He would go to the temple at Jerusalem and say, "I want twelve of your brightest young men to be my helpers. Give me some who have a high I.Q., are hard workers, and also are very handsome.

Instead, He chose ordinary working men who had not had any special religious training besides what they had received in their childhood and in the synagogue on the Sabbath.

This brings up a question. How about Judas? Was Jesus completely taken off guard by Judas' deception? Absolutely not! Jesus knew from the beginning who it was that would betray Him. Why pick him for an apostle, then, and even make him the treasurer? The answer – because it was the Father's will.

How does this relate to us today? God sees what is in our hearts today just as He did in Samuel's day. Psalm 139 points out God's perfect knowledge of us. He knows our thoughts and our words. He had a plan for our lives even before we were born.

Just as God picked David, I am glad that God picked me. My brothers made friends easily and they were fearless. I, on the other hand was shy and scared of my own shadow. God, however, looked beyond my flaws and imperfections because He knew I would come to love Him with all my heart.

GOD EMPOWERED DAVID TO DEFEAT THE GIANT.

The God who chooses is also the God who prepares and empowers us. David was, indeed, chosen to be the king, but that kingship was years in the future. 1st Samuel 16:13 tells us that after David was anointed, the Spirit of the Lord came upon him from that day forward.

Saul had been rejected by God, but he still continued to serve as king for many years. David had to wait upon God's timing. After learning that he was going to be the next king of Israel, he went back to his job of herding the family's sheep.

Before the battle with the Philistine ever came about, David was chosen to use his skill as a musician to minister to Saul. Saul had fits of madness that came upon him. David would play his lyre and the music would calm Saul down. Apparently, David made regular trips back and forth from Saul's house to his home in Bethlehem.

In 1st Samuel chapter 17 we find David again tending the sheep and Saul and the army fighting the Philistines. David's father asked him to go to where the army was and see how his brothers were.

When David got there, he heard the Philistine giant, Goliath, issue his challenge for hand-to-hand combat. The challenge was met with fear and trembling by everyone but David.

David was fearless.

Everyone else looked at the size of the giant. David looked at the size of his God. As we find out later in the story, while he was tending his father's sheep, he didn't let the threat of danger paralyze him. He overcame a lion and a bear that threatened the flock.

What made the difference? Why was everyone quaking with fear except David? The difference was his close personal relationship with God. He saw that God was being insulted by Goliath and he was indignant about it. A threat to his sheep was to be dealt with and a threat to the integrity of his God was also to be dealt with.

David was willing.

Many of us face situations in this life that we know are not right. We feel someone ought to do something about them. That someone, however, is not going to be us.

David expressed his willingness to go and fight the giant and word got to Saul. David was brought before him and Saul tried to talk him out of it. Saul pointed out very practical things, such as Goliath's size and his experience. David, though, with the eyes of faith looked beyond these obstacles. He saw the size of his God and the experience of his God. Then he told Saul about the lion and the bear who had tried to take one of his lambs. He gave God the credit for protecting him and giving him the victory.

What a disgrace this incident casts upon the whole Israelite army! Even if no one else was willing, Saul or his son, Jonathan, should have been willing. They had both experienced the power of God in giving victory against overwhelming odds. There were, undoubtedly, some brave men among the ranks but they were not willing. The only one willing was a teenager who was not even part of the army.

David was wise in his choice of weapons.

When Saul saw that he could not talk David out of going, he tried giving David his own armor. David tried the armor but rejected it almost immediately. He knew he had to fight the battle in his own way.

Instead of fighting Goliath in the traditional way, David used what he was familiar with – a slingshot. Not only was it something he was familiar with; it was something that Goliath would not expect. Goliath was all prepared to win an easy victory but God had other plans. 1ˢᵗ Samuel 17:49 says, *"And David put his hand in his bag and took out a stone and slung it and struck the Philistine on his forehead. The stone sank into his forehead, and he fell on his face to the ground."* Poor old Goliath! That rock was the last thing that entered his mind!

There is a spiritual lesson to be learned in this story. The lesson is this: you should not do God's work by using someone else's method or style. Do God's work in the way God leads you.

GOD PROTECTED DAVID FROM SAUL'S JEALOUSY.

The God who chose was the God who empowered and was also the God who protected. In Philippians 1:6 the apostle Paul expresses his assurance that the God who called a person to faith in the first place will see that faith grows and matures. It says, *"And I am sure of this, that He who began a good work in you will bring it to completion at the day of Jesus Christ."* In other words, if you invite Jesus to be your Lord and master, He is not ever going to abandon you.

At first, David was a hero and everyone was happy – including King Saul. Saul first made David his armor-bearer. Then he started sending him out as a commander of troops. God was with him and gave him success wherever he went. Instead of being pleased at this, Saul became jealous.

The incident that sparked Saul's jealousy in the first place is recorded in 1ˢᵗ Samuel 18:8 & 9. It was customary for women to meet the king with songs of victory. When these young women came out to meet the returning king, they sang a song which included this phrase: *"Saul has struck down his thousands and David his ten thousands."* Uh-oh! Trouble is brewing. Saul felt David was being honored more than he was.

It was not very long afterward that Saul tried to kill David by pinning him to the wall. Imagine going to work and fearing your boss would fly into a rage and try to kill you. Saul had moments when his sanity returned to him, but for the most part he was consumed by rage and jealousy. Finally, it became so bad David had to flee for his life. The rest of the book of 1st Samuel talks about Saul using his time and resources to pursue David and kill him. We can learn a couple of lessons from this record of David's hardship.

God used David's trials to strengthen his faith.

James 1:2 says, *"Count it all joy, my brothers, when you meet trials or various kinds, for you know that the testing of your faith produces steadfastness. And let steadfastness have its full effect, that you may be perfect and complete, lacking in nothing."*

Since the Christian life is a marathon instead of a sprint, we need to train for it so we don't quit in the middle of the race. The trials of life are part of the training.

There is a popular Christian song that reminds us it is easy to talk about faith when you are up on the mountain. The valley, however, is where our faith is proved to be the real thing. The song declares that the God of the mountain is also the God of the valley.

Many of the Psalms were written by David during his time of running from Saul. He was definitely in a situation that required God's help.

God became more real to David because he experienced the presence of God in his life.

One of my favorite T.V. cartoons is "Roadrunner". Wile E. Coyote is always trying to catch the roadrunner; but no matter what scheme he comes up with, he is never successful. This reminds me of King Saul trying to capture David.

At one time, when Saul and his men were closing in on David's small army a messenger came and told Saul the Philistines were raiding the country. Alas! Saul had to break off his hunt for David to go fight the real enemy.

On another occasion, Saul went into the very cave where David and his men were hiding. It would have been so easy to kill him at that point. But David would not lift a finger to put him to death. He knew that he was going to be king someday. He also knew that God would bring it about in His own way and His own time.

David had one member of the priestly family travelling with him and his men. Through that priest, David could get guidance from God about what to do in various situations.

I've got good news for you today. We don't need a priest to go to God on our behalf. We, as Christians, can go straight to God and pray for guidance. He can speak to us through His Word, through the Holy Spirit within us or through other Christians. Just as God delivered David from his trials, He can do the same for us.

GOD ESTABLISHED A COVENANT WITH DAVID.

2nd Samuel 7:1-16

All God's promises had come to pass. Saul and his son, Jonathan, were killed in battle. David became king over the tribe of Judah. Eventually he became king over the entire Israelite nation. At God's direction, he conquered the city of Jerusalem and set it up as the capital. He moved the ark of God to Jerusalem and he had a fine palace in which to live.

David's desire – to honor God by building a temple for Him.

David was now established as king and didn't have to worry about escaping from his enemies. He had an army to fight his battles and things were good. He knew it was God who had brought all these things to pass and wanted to honor Him. What better way was there to show honor than by building a magnificent structure to house the ark of God – the symbol of God's presence with His people.

David expressed his wish to Nathan, the prophet. Nathan, without praying about it or thinking it over, told David he thought it was a good idea.

God's response – "Thanks, but no thanks."

God spoke to Nathan that night and told him it was not His plan to have David build a temple for him. David was a man or war. His son, Solomon, would be a man of peace. It was David's son that would build the temple that David desired to build.

God's promise – a descendant who would have an everlasting throne – Jesus.

God had told Nathan that He did not want David to build a temple for Him. He revealed that it was Solomon who would do it. He also told David that He, Himself, would build a house for him. See 2nd Samuel 7:16 & 17. He was not talking about a physical house, but talking about a line of descendants who would bring forth a man named Jesus.

We see that God rewards faithfulness and obedience. God was the one who chose David, empowered him, protected him and established a covenant with him. We see this covenant played out in the New Testament where we find that Jesus is a descendant of David. The angel Gabriel told Mary that her son would reign over the house of Jacob forever.

As I look back over my life, I see God's hand in the experiences I've had. God chose me and guided me. Through my trials I've learned to depend on Him. As we face our trials, we might ask ourselves the question, "Am I reacting more like Saul or like David?"

Chapter 10

GOD DISCIPLINES HIS PEOPLE

Proverbs 3:11 & 12 *"My son, do not despise the Lord's discipline or be weary of His reproof, for the Lord reproves him whom He loves as a father the son in whom he delights."*

Hebrews 12:11 *"For the moment, all discipline seems painful rather than pleasant, but later it yields the peaceful fruit of righteousness to those who have been trained by it."*

I grew up with parents who abused me! They made all sorts of harsh demands on me. "Go to school." "Clean up your plate." "Do your chores." "Don't sass your mother." When I failed to live up to these things, they had no hesitation to apply the board of "education" to the seat of "learning."

They seemed to think that I would grow up to be a spoiled brat if it was left up to me. They were absolutely right. Guess what – God feels the same way. God realizes that part of love is discipline.

We think of discipline as negative, as the verse in Hebrews points out. Only as we look back on it can we see the benefit of discipline. Obedience brings blessings. Disobedience brings pain.

In the book of Deuteronomy, we see how this would play out in the life of the nation of Israel.

Obedience brings blessings. Deuteronomy 28:1-14

These are the blessings God promised for obedience:

1.) Dominance over other nations.

2.) Healthy children and healthy herds and flocks.

3.) Victory over enemies.

4.) Good crops.

5.) Rain at the proper time.

Disobedience is costly to you and those around you. Deuteronomy 28:15-53

These are the results of disobedience:

1.) Whatever you do won't succeed, whether you are a country boy or a city slicker.

2.) Sickly children, sickly herds and flocks.

3.) Poor crops.

4.) Confusion and frustration in all your projects.

5.) Lack of rain.

6.) Defeat by enemies.

7.) Sickness.

8.) Oppression and robbery by others.

9.) Exile from the land.

10.) Famine so bad that people resort to cannibalism!

Just in case you think that the people would never resort to cannibalism, read the story told in 2nd Kings 6:24-29 during a time of famine in Samaria.

WHAT IS THE BEST WAY TO REACT WHEN FACED WITH GOD'S DISCIPLINE?

We've seen that discipline is a sign of God's love for us. How do we respond to that discipline? What steps will make us **better** instead of **bitter**?

Pay attention to God's warning. Amos 4:6-11

There are many heroes in the Bible who set us a good example. We would all do well to have the patience of Job, the faithfulness of

Joshua or the courage of David. There are others, though, that give us an example of what NOT to do.

The prophet, Amos, was giving God's message to a hard-hearted, stiff-necked group of people who had paid no attention to God's warning.

In Amos 4:6-11, each verse ends with the refrain, "…yet you did not return to me," declares the Lord." The Lord used hunger, drought, poor harvest, pestilence and defeat by their enemies. In spite of all these things, the people never asked themselves, "Are all these things happening because I am sinning against God?"

God does not delight in lowering the boom on us. He tries to get our attention in many ways before He brings judgment. Cain was warned about his bad attitude long before he committed the world's first murder. King Saul was warned by the prophet Samuel but became resentful instead of seeing sin for what it was. God sent prophet after prophet to His people to warn them of what would happen to them, but they paid no attention.

Acknowledge our sin. Ezra 9:1-15

The people of Israel were warned over and over again not to enter into marriages with the Canaanites. God promised that if they ignored His prohibition, they would be exiled from the land. They not only inter-married – they started worshipping the idols their wives worshipped. Because of this, the temple in Jerusalem was destroyed, the city of Jerusalem was in ruins and many people were taken captive to Babylon.

Years later the Babylonians were conquered by the Persians. Cyrus, the king of Persia allowed the Jews to go back to Jerusalem and rebuild the temple. There were some that returned in 537 B.C.

In 458 B.C. a young priest named Ezra, who was an expert in the law of God, led a group back to Jerusalem. It says about him that Ezra had set his heart to **study** the Law of the Lord, and to **do** it and to **teach** God's law to his people. (Ezra 7:10)

When he got there, he found out the Jewish people were, again, involved in marriage with foreign women. What was so wrong about this practice? Is God prejudiced? Absolutely not! The problem was a spiritual one. The women were getting their husbands to worship the gods that they, themselves, worshipped. The Bible is not kidding when it says God is a jealous God. He does not share His majesty and glory with any man-made god.

Ezra 9:1-15 records Ezra's reaction to this news, and the prayer he prayed. He was heart-broken and asked for God's mercy upon the people. He included himself as a sinner, along with all the people. He was not involved in that particular sin, but he knew that he was just as prone to sin as everyone else.

Why was Ezra so grieved over others' sin? Maybe it was the fact that he loved God so much that he took sin seriously. If you love someone, you are grieved when others hurt them by words or deeds.

As a chaplain at a women prisoner's pre-release center, I can relate to his feeling of disappointment and frustration. I minister to women who seem to "get" the message, then make the same mistakes over and over again.

One day I saw two girls whom I thought I would never see locked up again. They were both thrilled to see me. I, on the other hand, was so upset to see them that I could hardly be civil. I felt like Ezra – tearing my hair out. Then I felt like Nehemiah – tearing their hair out! (See Nehemiah 13:25)

Therefore, the second step to benefit from God's discipline is to acknowledge our sin.

Learn from God's discipline. James 1:2-4

This brings up a question. When we are faced with hard times and trouble in our life, is it because we have sinned?

Not necessarily! It is good to look into our heart and see if there is a stubborn resistance to God's will. If our heart is right before God, however, we shouldn't blame ourselves for the trouble we face. I have known people who faced a life-altering illness and they have concluded that it was their own fault. Not so!

Our first question in the face of hard times should be, "Is God allowing this hardship because of my sin?" If we can see nothing standing in the way of fellowship with God, we should ask a different question. "Lord, what lesson can I learn from this? How can I use this to draw closer to you?"

According to James 1:2-4, God is interested in shaping our character. We can be obedient to God and still have a bad attitude. James says we should rejoice when we face trials because they can be used to build us into mature Christians. Remember, it takes time. The Christian life is a marathon, not a sprint.

Chapter 11

GOD RESTORES HIS PEOPLE

2ⁿᵈ Chronicles 6:24 & 25 "When your people Israel have been defeated by an enemy because they have sinned against you and when they turn back and confess Your name, praying and making supplication before you to this temple, then hear from heaven and forgive the sin of Your people Israel and bring them back to the land you gave to them and their fathers."

2ⁿᵈ Chronicles 7:14 "If my people, who are called by my name, will humble themselves and pray and seek My face and turn from their wicked ways, then will I hear from heaven and will forgive their sin and will heal their land."

The verses above show God's desire to bring His wayward people back into a right relationship with Him. The first verse was part of a prayer by Solomon at the dedication of the temple. The second verse is God's assurance that He had heard that prayer and would honor it.

In the last chapter we looked at the issue of God's discipline. Now in this chapter we will see the result that the discipline brought about. The people were allowed to go back to their own land.

The prophet, Jeremiah, predicted that the captivity of God's people in Babylon would last for seventy years. At the end of that time God would restore His people.

GOD WILL WORK IN OUR LIVES WHEN WE SEEK HIM WITH ALL OUR HEARTS.

Jeremiah had preached a message of warning and God's wrath upon Judah. Now, however, when that judgment had taken place, he turned to a message of comfort. The purpose of God's discipline is not to crush us and destroy us but to draw us back to Him. Jeremiah told the captives in Babylon that God still had plans for them.

Jeremiah 29:10-13 says, *"For thus says the Lord: When seventy years are completed for Babylon, I will visit you, and I will fulfill to you my promise and bring you back to this place. For I know the plans I have for you, declares the Lord, plans for welfare and not for evil, to give you a future and a hope. Then you will call upon me and come and pray to me and I will hear you. You will seek me and find me, when you seek me with all your heart."* (Emphasis mine.)

God promised to give His people a hope.

Without hope we give up. Because God promised it, we can depend on it. In our relationship with people, we don't put a lot of stock in promises. When God promises, though, we can bank on it.

God promised Abraham a son by his wife, Sarah. It seemed very unlikely that it would happen, but it finally did.

God promised the Israelites a land of their own when they left Egypt. It was this hope that kept Moses going in spite of the incredible obstacles in his path.

Throughout the Bible we have numerous promises made to us as Christians. Peter says, *"Blessed be the God and Father of our Lord Jesus Christ! According to His great mercy, He has caused us to be born again to a living hope through the resurrection of Jesus Christ from the dead."* 1st Peter 1:3

God promised to give His people a future.

For a great many people, the prospect of what will happen in the future fills them with dread and fear. We look at the state of the world and we despair. We worry about what might happen in the future and we despair.

What's the problem? We are concentrating on the wrong things. We are concentrating on our uncertainties rather than the sure and steadfast promises of God.

In these verses God is saying, in effect, "I'm not through with you yet." I wonder if Moses, during his forty years of keeping his father-in-law's sheep, concluded that God was finished with him. Surprise! God was preparing him for his real job.

We can take comfort from this. No matter how we have messed up, God is able to redeem us, restore us and use us for His glory. He's an expert in reconstruction.

God promised to hear their prayers.

2nd Chronicles chapter 33 tells the story of Manasseh, one of the kings of Judah. He began to reign at a very early age and spent most of his time undoing the good things that his father, Hezekiah, had done in Jerusalem. He built many altars, worshipped the moon and stars, abandoned the temple, and even practiced child sacrifice.

2nd Chronicles 33:10 says, *"The Lord spoke to Manasseh and his people, but they paid no attention."* Because of his failure to heed the voice of the Lord, he was taken captive to Babylon.

Once he was in captivity, he changed his mind and started praying to the God he had ignored all his life. 2nd Chronicles 33:13 records the result of that prayer. *"And when he prayed to Him, the Lord was moved by his entreaty and listened to his plea; so He brought him back to Jerusalem and to his kingdom."*

There are some amazing things in this story of king Manasseh. One of them is the disregard he had for God for many years of his reign. The other amazing thing is that once he had humbled himself, God heard his prayer.

Maybe you have been reluctant to pray because of your sinful past. This biblical example of God's mercy ought to be an encouragement to you to humble yourself and pray expectantly. God is not one to hold a grudge. He is quick to forgive.

Incidentally, the rest of the chapter tells how Manasseh took advantage of God's answer. He spent the rest of his life serving the true God instead of serving idols. In other words, it wasn't just a "jailhouse conversion." He had sincerely repented.

GOD WILL WORK IN OUR LIVES WHEN WE FOLLOW HIS PLAN.

The Babylonian kingdom fell to the Persians in 539 B.C. This new government was vastly different from the previous one. Cyrus, the Persian king issued a decree that allowed his Jewish captives to return to Jerusalem.

Ezra 1:1-3 "In the first year of Cyrus king of Persia, that the word of the Lord by the mouth of Jeremiah might be fulfilled, the Lord stirred up the spirit of Cyrus king of Persia, so that he made a proclamation throughout all his kingdom and also put it in writing. 'Thus says Cyrus king of Persia: The Lord, the God of heaven, has given me all the kingdoms of the earth, and he has charged me to build him a house at Jerusalem, which is in Judah. Whoever is among you of all his people, may his God be with him, and let him go up to Jerusalem, which is in Judah and rebuild the house of the Lord, the God of Israel – He is the God who is in Jerusalem."

God was at work by changings circumstances.

We are good at planning our lives, but we have no guarantee that things will work out as we planned. That is why we need to be flexible with regard to the future. James 4:13 & 14 says, *"Now listen, you who say, 'Today or tomorrow we will go to this or that city, spend a year there, carry on business and make money.' Why, you do not even know what will happen tomorrow. What is your life? You are a mist that appears for a little while and then vanishes. Instead, you ought to say, 'If it is the Lord's will, we will live and do this or that.' "*

So, does this mean we should just live day by day and take no thought for the future? By no means! We should plan for the future by asking for wisdom from God, who already knows what is going to happen. Since God knows our future, He can guide us into the path He wants us to follow.

The Israelites in Ezra's time had no idea, ten years before, that they would be allowed to return to Jerusalem. They never expected Babylon to be conquered and a new political power to arise. God was at work all the time. He is at work today arranging things in our lives, even though we might be totally unaware of it.

God was at work by changing the hearts of His people.

Two people can go to the same worship service and come away with totally different results. One will go away uplifted, encouraged and full of praise to God. The other will go away empty – empty of feeling, empty of praise and empty of hope.

What is the difference? Both heard the same songs. Both heard the same sermon. Both heard the same prayers. The difference is that in one case the words produce fruit because of the condition of the heart.

Jesus pointed this out in one of His first parables to the multitude. He talked about a farmer who sowed seed. Some of it fell along the path, some of it fell among rocky ground, some among thorny ground and some into good soil. Only the seed that fell into good soil produced any fruit. Jesus then went on to explain to His disciples that the soil was the condition of the heart.

I went to church, more out of habit than anything else. I had grown up going to church and continued after I got away from home. Eventually, I became critical of the church and stopped going. God, however, had not given up on me. He was at work, changing my heart.

The first change was my feeling of guilt over my sin. The second change was when I realized that all I had was a religion – not a relationship with Christ. The third change was a spiritual hunger to have that life-changing relationship with Jesus Christ.

In the lives of His people, God was working in their hearts to give them the desire to go back home. Now the time had come when that desire would fulfilled – because of the changed circumstances.

GOD WILL WORK IN OUR LIVES WHEN WE REPENT OF OUR SINS.

The return of the exiles did not happen all at once. It occurred over a number of years. The first return to Jerusalem was in 537 B.C.

The main purpose of the return was to rebuild the temple of God. They built an altar and laid the foundation of the new temple but stopped the work on it for a number of years. It was finally completed in 516 B.C. – 70 years after it had been destroyed.

80 years after the first group returned, there was a priest named Ezra who led a group back to Jerusalem. His purpose was to teach the law of God in Jerusalem.

15 years after Ezra had returned, there was a man named Nehemiah who led a group of people to Jerusalem. He was appointed by the king to be the governor over the Jewish people. His primary purpose was to rebuild the wall around Jerusalem. The wall was rebuilt in 52 days in spite of incredible opposition.

The physical deterioration was bad enough, but the spiritual deterioration was the real problem. They were no longer worshipping idols, but there was much disregard for the law of God. Nehemiah called everybody together and called upon Ezra to read the word of God and explain it to the people. Nehemiah 8:1-8 talks about that revival and verses 9-12 tells the result of hearing God's law.

Nehemiah 8:9-12 "And Nehemiah, who was the governor, and Ezra the priest and scribe, and the Levites who taught the people said to all the people, 'This day is holy to the Lord your God; do not mourn or weep.' For all the people wept as they heard the words of the Law. Then he said to them, 'Go your way. Eat the fat and drink sweet wine and send portions to anyone who has nothing ready, for this day is holy to our Lord. And do not be grieved, for the joy of the Lord is your strength.' So the Levites calmed all the people, saying, 'Be quiet, for this day is holy; do not be grieved.' And all the people went their way to eat and drink and to send portions and to make great rejoicing, because they had understood the words that were declared to them."

We see from this that repentance is not just feeling bad about our sin. It is feeling so bad that we turn from it and turn to God.

Repentance involves hearing what God says.

Hebrews 4:12 says, *"For the word of God is living and active, sharper than any two-edged sword, piercing to the division of soul and of spirit, of joints and of marrow, and discerning the thoughts and intentions of the heart."*

Many churches today don't let people know that they are dead in trespasses and sins. Instead, they emphasize the love of God and never mention the wrath of God. They want to put forth a positive message instead of a negative one.

We hear Jesus talking about God's love, but He also made it clear the people needed to repent of their sin. We need to hear about the judgment of God as well as the love of God.

Repentance involves doing what God says.

How many of you make New Year's resolutions? How many of you cast them aside by about January 15th? Repentance is being so disgusted by our sin that we find it impossible to continue in it.

For years after I was saved, I continued to smoke. Now, don't get me wrong. Smoking will not make you go to hell. It will just make you smell like you've been there. Nowhere in the Bible does it say, "Thou shalt not smoke."

The sin, for me, was not so much the smoking, but in trying to hide it. I became a liar and a hypocrite. I was professing to the world that I was trusting in God, but I was still a slave to my habit.

So, how did I finally overcome it? It was not until I had such a hunger to be close to God that I began to have the victory. My desire to obey God was stronger than my desire to continue in my sin.

Repentance involves a change of heart and mind.

How do we get this change of heart and mind? It takes daily doses of reading the Bible, memorizing scripture, meditating on what you read and praying for God to give you wisdom to carry it out in your life.

I've had many people over the years say to me, "I just don't feel as close to God as I used to." I usually respond with the story of the older couple who were driving down the street. The woman noticed the couple in the car ahead of them. They were cuddled up together as close as they could get. She said to her husband, "Look at them. That was the way we were, forty years ago." He thought for a moment and replied, "Well, I didn't move!" In other words, if you don't feel as close to God, who moved?

Chapter 12

GOD SENDS THE MESSIAH

Blessed be the God and Father of our Lord Jesus Christ, who has blessed us in Christ with every spiritual blessing in the heavenly places, even as He chose us in Him before the foundation of the world, that we should be holy and blameless before Him." Ephesians 1:3 & 4

"But when the fullness of time had come, God sent forth His Son, born of a woman, born under the law, to redeem those who were under the law, so that we might receive adoption as sons. Galatians 4:4 & 5

The verses above show that even before the world was created, God determined to send His Son to earth to take care of the sin problem of mankind. Before the first tree was created, God knew that one day a tree was to be cut down and made into a cross. These verses also show that God waited until just the right time to send the Son.

John chapter 1 talks about this Messiah that God sent. John called Him "the Word."

THE WORD OF GOD

John 1:1-5

Two basic questions arise. First, how do we know that this "Word" that John talks about is actually Jesus, the Son of God? We know it because John 1:14 makes it clear that the "Word became flesh and dwelt among us."

Second, why is Jesus called "the Word"? Simply because we use words to communicate with each other. Before Jesus came, God spoke to people in various ways. This whole book called the Bible is about the way God has revealed Himself to people throughout history.

God has never been one to play "hide and seek" with people. As a matter of fact, He has said, *"You will seek me and find me when you seek me with all your heart." Jeremiah 29:13* God has caused the Bible to be written, that we may know who He is. That is why He had prophets that would speak His words to the people. The prophets were not just spouting off their opinions when they spoke. Over and over again we find the words, "Thus says the Lord…"

At the time Jesus was born, there had not been a prophet in the land of Israel for over 350 years. It was as if God had said, "If you refuse to listen to me, I refuse to talk to you!" Now God was giving them another chance by sending Jesus. Every word Jesus spoke was at God's direction.

In the first chapter of the gospel of John we find three significant things about the Word.

He existed before the world began.

Verse 1 says, *"In the beginning was the Word, and the Word was with God and the Word was God."* Jesus was not a created being. At one time, in talking to the Jewish leaders, Jesus told them that He existed before Abraham was born. (John 8:58)

When God said in Genesis 1:26, *"Let us create man in our own image…"*, who is the "us"? It was Jesus and the Holy Spirit. The Hebrew word for God in Genesis 1 is "Elohim", a plural word. Jesus was born at a certain point in history but He has always existed as the Son of God.

He established the world.

John 1:3 says, *"All things were made through Him and without Him was not anything made that was made."* In other words, Jesus was active in the process of creation. He did not sit passively by and watch the Father do everything.

Jesus not only established the world, but He is the glue that holds it together. It is only by His grace and mercy that the world He created still exists for us to enjoy today.

He entered the world He created.

John 1:14 says, *"And the Word became flesh and dwelt among us..."* Imagine the glory that Jesus experienced at the right hand of the Father. He experienced close fellowship with the Father. He received the worship of the angels. He gazed on the beauty of heaven. He experienced the absence of sin, since it was heaven.

Now, imagine what it was like for Him to take on another form and be born as a human baby. Think of this – The "Word of God" couldn't speak a word when He was born. The one who had the power to put the sun and moon in place was completely dependent on a human couple for his every need. The one who received the worship of angels was destined to receive the scorn and hatred of men. The one who beheld the glory and splendor of heaven was born in a dirty barn.

That is what true love does. No sacrifice is too great. No gift is too costly. No pain is too much to bear.

THE WITNESS TO THE WORD

The gospel of Luke was written by a man who was not one of the apostles. Luke was a physician by trade and a companion of the apostle Paul. In the beginning of his gospel, Luke goes back before the birth of Jesus to talk about the birth of John the Baptist, the man who was to prepare the way for Jesus. (Luke chapter 1)

John's parents were Zechariah and Elizabeth. They were an older couple and a godly couple but they had no children. While Zechariah was burning incense in the temple, an angel appeared to him and announced that he and his wife were going to have a son. Zechariah was directed to name him John.

There were several things that the angel revealed to Zechariah about the son he would have. His son was prohibited from fermented drink, he would be filled with the Holy Spirit from birth, he would have a ministry like Elijah, and he was to prepare people for the coming of the Lord.

He was sent from God.

The last words of the Old Testament talk about God sending a specific individual to soften the hearts of people so that He could deal with them in mercy rather than dealing with them in wrath. Malachi 4:5 & 6 says, *"See, I will send you the prophet Elijah before the great and dreadful day of the Lord comes. He will turn the hearts of the fathers to their children and the hearts of the children to their fathers; or else I will come and strike the land with a curse."*

In these verses, when God says He will send the prophet Elijah, it does not mean that He will send Elijah back to earth (although He could do that.) It means that He will send someone that will be like Elijah. He will be bold and fearless and will lead people to repent of their sin.

In Luke 1:17, the angel uses the exact same words in describing the ministry of John the Baptist. He was one sent before the Lord to prepare the way for Jesus.

Who was Elijah? He was the prophet who confronted the wicked king of Israel and predicted a drought. After three and a half years he appeared to the king again and called for a public contest to see who was really God – the God he worshipped, or Baal, the god of the Canaanites. God was the one who answered by fire and Baal was proved to be a false and powerless object of worship.

Luke 1:80 says about John, *"And the child grew and became strong in spirit; and he lived in the desert until he appeared publicly to Israel."*

He didn't take any glory or credit for himself.

When John began his ministry, it caused a stir among the people. For hundreds of years there had not been a prophet of the Lord among them. Now, all of a sudden, here was someone preaching boldly and fearlessly and exhorting them to repent of their sin.

The word about this Baptizer spread. Eventually the word got to Jerusalem, the center of Jewish worship. Jerusalem was where the temple was. Jerusalem was the home of the religious elite. They knew a lot about God, thus thinking they were the smartest people and the most righteous people in the world.

When they heard of this new preacher, they sent a delegation to check out his credentials. John 1:19-27 tells of John's conversation with the delegation from Jerusalem.

First, they asked him if he was the Messiah. Every Jewish person was aware that God would someday send a Messiah who would be their leader. They were, however, expecting a military leader and not a spiritual one. He responded that he was not the Messiah.

Then, they asked him if he was Elijah. They were aware of God's promise in Malachi. John told them he was not Elijah.

They asked him if he was "the prophet." Again, he gave them a negative answer.

They then asked him what he had to say about himself. He said, *"I baptize with water, but among you stands one you do not know. He is the one who comes after me, the thongs of whose sandals I am not worthy to untie." John 1:23*

There were others that wondered if he was the Christ. He was quick to point to his servant role and let them know that Christ was much greater than himself. He described Christ as the bridegroom and himself as just the bridegroom's friend.

He pointed others to Christ.

As we follow along in the first chapter of John's gospel, we see John pointing others to Christ. One day John saw Jesus coming toward him and pointed Him out to the crowd as the "lamb of God" who would take away the sin of the world.

The next day John was with two disciples and again saw Jesus. He again called Him "The lamb of God." The two disciples followed Jesus and ended up spending the day with Him. They became disciples of Jesus instead of disciples of John. Instead of feeling jealous and resentful, John was perfectly happy with this development.

This should be our attitude toward the job God has given us to do. Our job is not to make disciples for ourselves. Our job, like John's, is to make disciples for Jesus.

THE WORLD'S REACTION TO THE WORD

You would think that the ones who were most familiar with scripture would be eagerly awaiting the fulfillment of God's promise to send a Savior to them. They were! The problem was that they had their own idea of what that Savior should be like.

There were many Old Testament scriptures that talked about Jesus. Some talked about His meekness, humility and suffering. Others talked about His power, authority and glory. What they did not understand was that it talked about two comings of the same person. The first coming was in weakness, the second coming was in glory and power. They were separated by thousands of years.

Not understanding God's plan, these "experts" in the law of God concentrated on the "power" verses and ignored the "weakness" verses.

Sometimes we do the same the same thing with the Word of God. We concentrate on God's love and completely ignore the fact that God hates sin.

They did not recognize Him.

John 1:10 says, *"He was in the world, and though the world was made through him, the world did not recognize Him."* Why didn't they recognize Him?

Maybe it was because He was an ordinary human being, just like they were. All they could see was that He was a good teacher, a great miracle-worker and a kind person – but just a person, nevertheless. Jesus didn't have a halo around His head. He was not a John Wayne – type individual.

When He went to His hometown after beginning His ministry, his friends and neighbors listened in amazement as He explained the scripture. They wondered where He had gotten such learning. They thought about His family, and there was nothing remarkable about them. They thought about the fact that they grew up with Him. The hometown people did not recognize Him because He was too common.

The high muckety-mucks of the Jewish religion didn't recognize Him because He did not fill their picture of what the Messiah should be like. He came as a spiritual leader and not a military one. They did not recognize Him because they did not recognize their sin.

They did not receive Him.

There were all kinds of people who came to Jesus for one reason or another and went away with their lives unchanged and their hearts untouched.

One, especially, was a sincere young man who came to Jesus and asked what he had to do to receive eternal life. Jesus cited some commandments and the man declared he had kept them. Jesus then instructed him to sell all he had, give it to the poor and come follow Him. The man could not bring himself to do this and he went away sad. Think of how tragic this was. He came to the right source. He asked the right question. Then he made the wrong response.

Even one of the disciples, Judas, followed Him but didn't receive Him. It is not enough to know about Jesus. We must accept His lordship in our life.

They did not realize their spiritual need.

In Luke 18:9-14 Jesus told a parable about two men who went to the temple to pray. Verse 9 tells the reason Jesus told the parable. *"To some who were confident of their own righteousness and looked down on everybody else, Jesus told this parable."*

The first character was a very religious individual who tried as hard as he could to keep all the rules and regulations of his religion. He is called a Pharisee. The Pharisees made up many rules and customs in order to keep God's law. The trouble with this man is that he did not see that pride is a sin and contempt of others is a sin. In his "prayer" to God he reminded God of how good he was, especially compared to "that tax-collector."

The second character was the tax collector. He was painfully aware of his sin and asked God for mercy. His attitude before God was humility. Jesus says that this man was the one who went home justified.

Jesus went on to say that everyone who exalts himself will be humbled, and he who humbles himself will be exalted.

We need to recognize our sin, repent of our sin and receive Jesus as our Savior.

Chapter 13

MAKING IT PERSONAL

John 1:12 "Yet, to all who received Him, to those who believed in His name, He gave the right to become children of God."

John 3:16 "For God so loved the world that He gave His one and only Son, that whoever believes in Him shall not perish but have eternal life."

The life and ministry of Jesus proves the truth of the statement in Isaiah, *" 'For my thoughts are not your thoughts, neither are your ways my ways' declares the Lord." Isaiah 55:8.*

God does things in totally unexpected ways. For example, who would expect the one who could heal blindness, lameness and leprosy to grow up in a backwards country town of Nazareth?

Who would expect the mighty Son of God to have to work for a living – to get His hands dirty working with wood and stone?

More than that, when He started calling disciples, who would think that He would call the flawed, spiritually dull disciples He ended up with. Why not go to the temple in Jerusalem and announce that He was looking for twelve of their brightest students?

That, however, was not Jesus' way. Instead, he called a rag-tag band of followers. A casual reading of the gospels reveals their glaring imperfections. They were continually misunderstanding Him. Some of them were hot-tempered. They were always arguing with one another. One was doubting. Another was inconsistent. One became a traitor. How was Jesus going to soar with eagles while working with this bunch of turkeys? Simple – purely through the grace of God which would transform 11 of them into what God had designed them to be. (This is the same grace that is offered to us today.)

Toward the end of His time on earth, Jesus led His disciples to a place outside of Jewish territory. Then He began to question them about their understanding of Him and the implications of that understanding for their life. The story is told in Matthew 16:13-27

CONFESSION OF CHRIST AS LORD

This is where it all starts! Jesus is our only hope. Jesus told His disciples in John 14:6 that He was THE way, THE truth and THE life. NO ONE came to the Father except through Him.

He started out with a general question. "Who do people say that I am?" There were many different opinions, as there are today.

Because of His authoritative way of teaching, some thought that He was one of the great Old Testament prophets that had been raised from the dead. This might seem far-fetched to us, but not to them. They were aware of the power of God and some of them believed in the resurrection. To them, this was entirely within the realm of possibility.

Regardless of whether they held Him in high esteem or not, all answers fell short of the right answer.

The disciples gave their answers as to what people were saying about Jesus. Then Jesus turned to a specific question. "How about you, personally? What do you say?" Peter, of course, was the one who came up with the right answer. Jesus was the Son of the living God. Confession of Christ as Lord is the starting place in salvation. We can see three things about Peter's statement.

It was a personal decision.

Each one of us must make a personal decision for ourselves. We can't get into heaven on someone else's coattails.

Years ago, we were involved in trying to establish a church. I went to introduce myself and meet people in the area. I called upon a young couple who invited me in. After a short time of general conversation, I asked the man if he had a relationship with Christ. He replied, "My wife takes care of the religion in our household."

"In other words," I replied, "you're telling me that when you die and stand before God, He asks you why He should let you into His heaven, that you're going to say, 'I thought my wife took care of that.' "

He had no answer to that. Hopefully, I gave him some food for thought that would change his life.

Like Jesus' first question to the disciples, it makes no difference what someone else thanks about Jesus. The only thing that makes a difference is what YOU think.

It was a spiritual decision.

Jesus commended Peter for coming up with the right answer. He did not, however, say that it was the result of his intellect or of doing his homework. It was because it was revealed to him by the Spirit of God. 1st Corinthians 1:18 says, *"For the message of the cross is foolishness to those who are perishing, but to us who are being saved it is the power of God."*

It was Peter who gave the answer, but I believe he was speaking for the group (with the exception of Judas.) Why did the disciples get it right? Why did the religious leaders get it wrong? Could it have been that the disciples were open to new learning and the religious leaders were not? Their minds were filled with scripture and their hearts were proud of their knowledge. They were not open to learning because they thought they knew it all. The Bible says God gives grace to the humble but resists the proud.

It was a life-changing decision.

The disciples' life did not change right away. They still had lapses of faith. They still had selfish motives. They still had misunderstandings. But that confession of Christ as Lord was the entrance into the place of blessings that God wanted to give them.

For me, it was a memorable experience when I confessed Jesus as Lord. I gave Him an invitation to invade my life when I said, "Take over, Lord!" Immediately I had an awareness that my sins had been forgiven. I was filled with the knowledge that Jesus was the one I was going to be following for the rest of my life.

I had moved from death into life, from darkness into light, and from a religion to a relationship with the Savior.

Keep in mind, though, that it does not affect everybody the same way. Some people are emotional about it and others are not. If you have sincerely asked Jesus to be your Savior from sin and to be the Lord of your life, He will not refuse that request. As a matter of fact, He gives assurance of this in Revelation 3:20. *"Here I am! I stand at the door and knock. If anyone hears my voice and opens the door, I will come in and eat with him and he with Me."*

As we follow the story in Matthew 16, we see that after giving the right answer as to the identity of Jesus, Peter gave the wrong response as to God's agenda.

CONFLICT WITH GOD'S AGENDA

As soon as Jesus informed His followers what was in store for Him in Jerusalem, Peter objected to it.

Rebuking Christ

We don't like change. Peter was no different than we are. Even if life has its rough spots, we want to stay with the familiar instead of launching into an uncertain future.

It must have been fulfilling for the disciples to follow Jesus day after day. Imagine what it would be like to hear Him make the Word of God plain. Imagine what it would be like to see Him heal multitudes of people. Imagine what it was like to witness His love.

Now He was telling them plainly that things were going to be different. No wonder they were upset.

Peter took it upon himself to let Christ know that He ought not to talk that way. He was discouraging His disciples. What he said, in effect was, "We're not going to let anything happen to You. In today's language, "We've got your back!" How foolish for Peter and his companions to think they could protect Christ from an angry mob.

This was not the first time that a human being had tried to tell the Son of God what He should or should not do. We find it all through the gospels.

In John, chapter 2 it tells of Jesus performing the first of His miracles. He and His disciples were at a wedding celebration. Jesus' mother came to Him and told Him that they were out of wine. I believe that she was hoping He would use His power as the Son of God to remedy the situation. Although Jesus did perform the miracle of turning water into wine, He had to remind His mother that He was under the authority of His heavenly Father. He was no longer under her authority.

John, chapter 7 tells of His brothers asking Him why He didn't go to Jerusalem and perform some miracles. It goes on to say that they did not believe in Him as the Christ.

His disciples were notorious for telling Him what He should do. "Send the crowd away." "Get these children out of here." "We're perishing! Do something!"

Rebuked by Christ

Usually, Jesus was very patient with His disciples. He took time to explain parables to them. He put up with their silly arguments. He led them gently upon the path of righteousness. In this case, however, Jesus issued a stinging rebuke. It was not gentle or kind at all. Matthew 16:23 says Jesus turned and said to Peter, *"Get behind me, Satan! You are a stumbling block to Me; you do not have in mind the things of God, but the things of men."*

The Bible says that our thoughts are not God's thoughts nor are our ways His ways. Peter was looking at things from a merely human perspective. He was totally unaware of the glorious plan of God that would take care of the sin problem. That plan would result in glory, but must first involve suffering.

CONDITIONS FOR DISCIPLESHIP

Jesus then laid out the conditions for being His followers. Matthew 16:24 says, *"Then Jesus said to His disciples, 'If anyone would come after me, he must deny himself and take up his cross and follow me.' "*

We see, then, that discipleship is not a bed of roses but a hard road. There are three things involved in discipleship.

Deny yourself.

What does it mean to deny yourself? Does it mean that you have to deny yourself every form of comfort in the world? That is what a number of hermits in the third century thought. They were so troubled by the temptations of the world that they went out into the desert and lived in caves. There were some who ate very little and some who were very eccentric in their behavior.

If denying yourself consists of getting rid of all pleasures and comforts, I have really blown it out of the water. I have comfortable furniture in my house. I drive a car that is comfortable. I have things in life that I enjoy doing that are not necessarily spiritual. I eat food that I enjoy.

I believe that Jesus' command to deny ourselves is to keep these things we enjoy from becoming a stumbling block to serving God. "I know I ought to be in church tonight, but my favorite T.V. show is on." "Sunday is the only day I get to sleep in." "I know I ought to be in church but today is a perfect day for…" We need to thank God for the things we enjoy in life, but don't let them become our "gods".

Take up your cross.

There is often misunderstanding about taking up your cross Many people look at their cross as some drudgery in life they have to put up with. This is not what Jesus means by taking up our cross.

Taking up our cross is willingly and obediently carrying out the job God has given us to do. For Jesus, it was a literal cross. That was what God had assigned Him to do. For most of the disciples it was a martyr's death. For many of the early Christians it was the same.

What does "taking up your cross" mean for you? It means doing the job God has assigned you to do. Ephesians 2:10 says, *"For we are God's workmanship, created in Christ Jesus to do good works, which God prepared in advance for us to do."*

Follow Me.

This is a straight-forward command. What part of it do you not understand?

There were some who wanted to follow Jesus, but didn't. There was a rich young man who sincerely wanted eternal life. Jesus told him to give away his wealth and follow Him. He could not bring himself to do that because the cost was too great. Jesus wants an all-out commitment.

In Luke 9:57-62 we see what type of dedication Jesus requires. The first man had an emotional response to Jesus. Jesus wants a well-thought-out commitment. The second man couldn't follow right then. Jesus wants an immediate commitment. The third man was willing to follow, but his heart was divided. Jesus wants an undivided commitment.

What is stopping you from following Jesus? Remember when you asked Him to be your Savior and Lord? If He is not Lord OF all, He is not Lord AT all.

Imagine Jesus coming to your home. You welcome Him gladly, invite Him in and tell Him to make Himself at home. Then you tell Him, "Don't go into that closet over there." "Stay out of the refrigerator." This is what it is like being a Christian that does not follow Jesus. He is welcome as long as He doesn't interfere with your lifestyle.

Chapter 14

BECAUSE HE LIVES

John 12:24 "I tell you the truth, unless a kernel of wheat falls to the ground and dies, it remains only a single seed. But if it dies, it produces many seeds."

Matthew 28: 5 & 6 "The angel said to the women, 'Do not be afraid, for I know that you are looking for Jesus, who was crucified. He is not here; he has risen, just as he said. Come and see the place where he lay.' "

Would you like to know when, where and how you are going to die? I have asked this question to numerous people during my ministry and have received very few "yes" answers. Most of us prefer that death be a mystery until it happens.

To Jesus, however, it was not a mystery. He knew even before He began His ministry that He was destined to die an agonizing death on a hill outside of Jerusalem. He knew when it would happen. He knew where it would happen. He knew why it would happen – because He would be betrayed by one of His followers.

A SHAMEFUL DEATH

Crucifixion was one of the worst ways for a person to die. One reason is that it was a slow death. Some people lasted for two or three days.

Crucifixion was not only excruciatingly painful but it was shameful and humiliating. It was done in a public place where there were many passersby. The other shameful thing about it was that the victim was entirely naked. Nudity was a disgrace, especially for Jewish people.

In spite of His pain and His public humiliation, Jesus took the time to minister to others. Let us consider Jesus' words from the cross.

A word of mercy and grace.

Luke 23:34 "Jesus said, 'Father, forgive them, for they do not know what they are doing."

In spite of all the hard-heartedness and stubbornness of the people He was trying to minister to, Jesus was not filled with bitterness and anger. He was, instead, filled with compassion because they were like sheep who were without a shepherd. Even in the extremities of his agony, He was still concerned with their souls.

A word of assurance to the repentant thief.

Luke 23:43 "Jesus answered him, 'I tell you the truth, today you will be with me in paradise."

There were three crosses on that hill that day. Two thieves were crucified with Jesus. At first, both of them mocked Jesus, right along with the crowd. The one thief wanted Jesus to prove His power by getting all of them out of their dire situation – so like people today who want to use God as a lucky charm. Just rub the bottle the right way and get your wishes granted!

As time went on, however, one thief realized the love Jesus showed and decided He was really who He said He was – the Son of God. At that moment he did the only thing he could do, which was to cast himself on the mercy of Jesus. He said, "Remember me when you come into your kingdom."

WHAT???? Do you mean to tell me that rascal is today enjoying the glories of heaven? THAT'S NOT FAIR!!!! No, it's not fair – it's mercy! If it was fairness we wanted, nobody would be in heaven.

A word of care.

John 19:26 & 27 "When Jesus saw his mother there, and the disciple whom he loved standing nearby, He said to His mother, 'Dear woman, here is your son,' and to the disciple, 'Here is your mother.' From that time on, this disciple took her into his home."

As the oldest son, Jesus was responsible for the welfare of His mother. After the return of the family to Nazareth, Joseph is never mentioned again in scripture. The assumption is that he had already died. Jesus was concerned with how His mother would get along and He assigned her care to one whom He knew would be faithful to care for her.

A word of anguish.

Matthew 27:46 "About the ninth hour Jesus cried out in a loud voice, 'Eloi, Eloi, lama sabachthani' which means, 'My God, My God, why have you forsaken me?' "

For a brief period of time, God could not look upon the Son whom He loved. He, who had been at the Father's side throughout eternity, He who was separated from the Father during His time on earth, was now forsaken by His Father because the ugliness of sin was so great that Father could not bear to look at it.

We have undoubtedly have had times in our life when we feel like God has forsaken us, but it simply is not true. God hasn't moved. That is just the way we feel. In Jesus' case, however, the abandonment was real. Real – but temporary.

Read Psalm 22 and see how many verses describe what Jesus went through on that old rugged cross.

A word of human need.

John 19:28 "Later, knowing that all was now completed, and so that the Scripture would be fulfilled, Jesus said, 'I am thirsty.' "

Jesus, as fully man, experienced the same things in His life as we do in ours. He got tired. He needed sleep. He was angry. He was hungry. He was thirsty. Since He experienced all these things, He can understand when we go through the same things. He is a God of all comfort.

A word of surrender.

Luke 23:46 "Jesus called out with a loud voice, 'Father, into your hands I commit my spirit.' "

During His life, Jesus had developed the habit of always surrendering to the Father. That's why, when He faced the ordeal of the cross, He could say, "Father, not my will, but yours be done." He taught His followers to say the same thing in what we recite today as the Lord's prayer. "Thy will be done on earth as it is in heaven."

A word of victory.

John 19:30 " When He had received the drink, Jesus said, 'It is finished.' With that, he bowed his head and gave up his spirit."

What did Jesus mean by "it is finished"? Did He mean His life was finished? Did He mean His ministry was finished? Did He mean His pain was finished? All these things were true, but I think He meant something greater. I believe He was talking about God's plan for dealing with the sin of the human race. Even back in Genesis 3:15 God made a promise that someone would come to deal with the curse of sin. Satan's plan was foiled. God won, through the obedience of Jesus, the lamb of God, who came to take away the sin of the world.

A GLORIOUS RESSURECTION.

What a difference the appearance of Jesus made in the lives of two disciples who were on their way to the village of Emmaus! These two were on their way home. Their leader had died and their hopes had died with Him. The Bible tells us that the town they were going to was seven miles from Jerusalem. Now, seven miles does not seem like a great distance to us, but it probably would if we had to walk it.

Luke 24:13-35 tells us the story of their conversation with the risen Jesus.

They were walking along, talking about these horrible events which had befallen their beloved Jesus. Suddenly the risen Lord appeared and started walking with them. The Bible goes on to say that they were kept from recognizing Him. To them, He was just a fellow-traveler who happened to be going the same way.

Jesus asked them what they had been talking about. They responded, "About the things that have happened in Jerusalem." Then they proceeded to tell Him about the crucifixion. Along with the facts, they related their reaction to what had happened. Their hopes were dashed. Moreover, they were puzzled by reports of the missing body.

Luke 24:25 &26 "Jesus said to them, 'O foolish ones, and slow of heart to believe all that the prophets have spoken! Was it not necessary that the Christ should suffer these things and enter into His glory?' "

Then Jesus proceeded to give them a Bible study concerning the verses in the Old Testament which spoke of the Christ that would come. Perhaps He quoted the verse in Isaiah which speaks of being born of a virgin. Maybe He went on to explain Isaiah 53, which talks about the death of the Savior. I'll bet He used the verse in Micah, which talks about Him being born in Bethlehem.

In other words, sending a Savior to pay for sins was not just an idea that God thought up after many years. The Old Testament speaks of a need for sacrifice. Each sacrifice was a picture of the perfect sacrifice to come – the Lamb of God which takes away the sin of the world.

As they approached the town, Jesus acted as if He were going to go on down the road. Why would He do that? I believe that He wanted to give the two men an opportunity to give Him an invitation. Jesus loves to accept invitations, but He does not barge in where He is not wanted. The invitation has to come from us. Revelation 3:20 talks about Jesus knocking on the door of our heart. But we have to be the ones who open the door.

When they sat down to supper, Jesus did an unusual thing. It was supposed to be the host that would distribute the bread for the meal. In this case, Jesus assumed the role of the host. It was He who broke the bread.

That was when the men's eyes were opened and they recognized it was Jesus, Himself. What a thrill that must have been as they realized that what the women were saying was true after all.

Although it was now dark, they could not wait to go back the seven miles to Jerusalem to tell the other disciples. How different was Sunday from Friday! Consider what had been opened to them in the space of a few short hours.

Their minds were opened.

During the course of Jesus' explanation of the scriptures that told about Him, the disciples had a new understanding.

My time at a Bible College was one of the most enjoyable times in my life. I was eager to learn, and the teachers made the scriptures come alive. There were some courses that were incredibly boring. For the most part, however, it was an enriching experience. This is likely how those two disciples felt.

Their eyes were opened.

Luke 24:16 tells us specifically that they were kept from recognizing Him. I believe it was God, Himself, who kept them from recognizing this stranger as Jesus. If they had recognized Him, they would likely have been so overwhelmed that they wouldn't have heard a word He said to them.

It was only when Jesus had finished what He had to say to them that their eyes were opened. Luke 24:30 & 31 says, *"When He was at the table with them, He took bread, gave thanks, broke it and began to give it to them. Then their eyes were opened and they recognized Him and He disappeared from their sight."*

Their hearts were opened.

As soon as the resurrected Jesus was revealed to them, the two disciples talked with each other about their innermost feelings. They testified that their hearts were "burning within them" as Jesus explained the scripture.

I grew up going to church on a regular basis. I never doubted that God existed. I knew that Jesus had died for my sin. I believed in heaven and hell. I had an intellectual belief but my heart was dead and cold.

I recall going to church camp one year and standing before an old wooden cross. I knew that I should feel love for Jesus. I knew that I should feel grateful. What bothered me on that day was that I felt – nothing!

It was not until I surrendered my life to the Lord twelve years later, that "my heart burned within me." That is the kind of heartburn that only God can create. That is a "holy heartburn."

Their mouths were opened.

When they recognized the living Lord, they were filled with hope instead of despair. The attitude was one of excitement.

I can relate to this. When I uttered the words, "Take over, Lord!", I was inviting God to help Himself to my life. All of a sudden, I wanted to tell everybody about it.

The two disciples were the same way. They had just walked seven miles. Now it was night-time and they couldn't wait to get back to Jerusalem and tell their friends.

What a difference it makes in a life when God becomes real and personal to you. It opens up a whole new spiritual world.

A LIVING HOPE

1st Peter 1: 3 & 4 says, *"Praise be to the God and Father of our Lord Jesus Christ! In his great mercy He has given us new birth into a living hope through the resurrection of Jesus Christ from the dead, and into an inheritance that can never perish, spoil or fade kept in heaven for you…"*

The same thought is expressed in a song by Bill and Gloria Gaither. The song is called, "Because He Lives". The central message of the song is that because of the resurrection we can face the uncertainties in life. We can face the heartbreak. We can face the discouragements. We can face the death of loved ones. As I write these words, I am looking at a picture of my son. He was seven years old when he was hit by a car and killed instantly. How can I bear this loss? Only because Jesus' resurrection proved that death is not the end. Death is the entrance into a life that never ends.

Our reservation in heaven is secure.

Several years ago, my wife and I went on an extended trip, which involved making motel reservations. At one place we stopped, they did not have the "non-smoking" room I requested. They gave us a room that had the odor of stale smoke.

Reservations are great, but are prone to human error. Not so with our reservation in heaven. The moment we put our trust in Jesus, our name is written in the Lamb's book of life.

There are two books in heaven that determine our destiny. One is the Lamb's Book Of Life. If our name is written there, our entrance to heaven is guaranteed. If our name is not there, we are judged out of the book of works. For a discussion of these things, see Revelation 20:11-15.

Our salvation includes the "now" and the "then".

Do you remember going on a trip as a family? The kids would ask repeatedly, "Are we almost there?" To a kid, everything that doesn't happen right away takes too long. Sometimes we, as Christians, feel the same way.

We think of all the glories of heaven and experience the trials of this life. We think of the perfect relationships we will have in heaven and experience the bitterness of marred relationships on earth. We think of sweet fellowship with the Savior and experience times of spiritual drought and dryness in our lives.

The Christians life is described as a race. Hebrews 12:1 says, *"Therefore, since we are surrounded by such a great cloud of witnesses, let us throw off everything that hinders and the sin that so easily entangles, and let us run with perseverance the race marked out for us."*

Considering all these things, what is so great about being a Christian in the "here" and "now"? Simply this – that the Christian has the Spirit of the living God within them. Jesus said He came, that people may have life and have it more abundantly. (See John 10:7-10)

When I made my decision to surrender my life to Jesus, it was as if I came alive. Each day was filled with eagerness and excitement instead of frustration and drudgery.

We are not immune to trials that grow our faith.

When I think of trials that grow our faith, I usually think of the apostle, Paul. Now, there was a man who had problems.

After Christ appeared to him and Paul accepted Him as Lord, the persecution started almost immediately. He had to sneak out of Damascus to avoid being killed. That was only the beginning. It got worse and worse. Everywhere Paul went, he was either beaten, stoned or run out of town.

Just one example: when he went to the city of Philippi (at the direction of the Lord.) He cast an evil spirit out of a slave girl, thus incurring the wrath of her owners. They had Paul and Silas severely beaten. That was bad enough, but after the beating they were put in the jail with their feet fastened in stocks.

We don't have to wonder what their attitude was during this painful and unjust treatment. According to the story recorded in Acts 16, they were singing hymns and praising God!

Didn't they have some doubts and questions during that time? Didn't they ever question whether it was worth it to follow the Lord? The Bible does not address that question. Even if they did have doubts, their faith won out.

This story does have a happy ending, though. God ended up showing His mighty power. Lives were changed, and a church was started in that city.

1ˢᵗ Peter 4:12 & 13 says, *"Dear friends, do not be surprised at the painful trial you are suffering, as though something strange were happening to you. But rejoice that you participate in the sufferings of Christ, so that you may be overjoyed when his glory is revealed."*

Chapter 15

THE WORK CONTINUES

John 14:12 "I tell you the truth, anyone who has faith in me will do what I have been doing. He will do even greater things than these, because I am going to the Father."

Power when the Holy Spirit comes on you; and you will be my witnesses in Jerusalem, and in all Judea and Samaria, and to the ends of the earth."

What would happen when Jesus left the earth and went back to heaven? Sometimes in life it seems to us that certain people are absolutely essential and we couldn't possibly get along without them. We had an assistant pastor at the church I attend. He was a wonderful musician, a great preacher, and I thought, numerous times, how blessed we were to have him. The time came when he was called to another church. In the meantime, a young man and his family had joined the church. He, too, was a wonderful musician. He stepped right in to lead the worship service. One person was called away, but God had another person waiting in the wings.

The disciples must have felt devastated. Jesus was no longer going to be on earth. What was going to happen to the work He began? Who was going to explain the Old Testament scriptures and tell the good news about forgiveness of sin? Never fear! God still had a plan.

JESUS INSTRUCTED THE APOSTLES.

As joyful as the apostles were when they realized that Jesus had risen, they were still unprepared for what was to come. They still had an incomplete understanding. Their question to Him about restoring the kingdom to Israel shows they misunderstood God's plan.

Therefore, Jesus used the time He spent with them to shape their thinking and prepare their hearts. During this time, Jesus gave His apostles three definite things.

He gave them proof of His resurrection.

The Bible says that He appeared to them on multiple occasions. He appeared to them in the upper room on at least two occasions. He appeared to the two disciples on the way to Emmaus. He appeared to them on their fishing trip on the Sea of Galilee. He let them touch Him. He ate with them. He talked with them. Paul said he appeared to a group of 500 people, at some point.

How many times have you seen a headline in a "less-than-reputable" newspaper about Elvis still being alive? Or a severely brain-damaged John Kennedy being secluded in some place? Where is the proof? It is not there, although many people believe it.

The disciples had an abundance of evidence, because they needed to be absolutely convinced of the truth. The persecution they endured was so severe that their faith in the resurrection was the only thing that carried them through. They would not have given their lives for a hoax.

He gave them a promise of the Holy Spirit.

We find that there is such a thing as a Holy Spirit in Genesis Chapter 1. Verse 2 says, *"the Spirit of God was hovering over the face of the waters."*

As we progress through the Old Testament, we find the Spirit coming upon different individuals to empower them to do God's will. God's Spirit was at work all through the time before Christ came. Now, Jesus told the disciples that the Holy Spirit would come in a new power and fullness.

Then Jesus told them something that none of us likes to hear – wait! They had to wait because they did not have the power which the Holy Spirit would give. They had to wait because they didn't have the knowledge of the Old Testament scriptures. The Holy Spirit would give them that knowledge. They had to wait because they were weak and frail human beings. The Holy Spirit would fill them with boldness. Instead of being fearful, they became fearless.

He gave them a picture of His plan for them.

His disciples had a misconception about God's plan. This is shown by the question they asked Jesus. Acts 1:6 says, *"So when they had come together, they asked Him, 'Lord, will you at this time restore the kingdom to Israel?' "*

That was when Jesus gave them a picture of His plan for them. He told them they wouldn't know when that day would come. In the meantime, they were to continue the work to which He had called them.

He told them they would be His witnesses in Jerusalem, in all Judea and Samaria, and to the ends of the earth. In other words, He wanted them to start in Jerusalem and then spread out to the surrounding areas. His plan for them was to spread the news about Him wherever they went. What an awesome responsibility! No wonder they had to wait until the Spirit came upon them.

THE HOLY SPIRIT ENABLED THE APOSTLES.

The Jewish people celebrated several festivals during the year. If possible, Jewish people in all locations would make their way to Jerusalem to celebrate these festivals.

One of the important festivals was the Feast of Pentecost. It occurred fifty days after the Passover. Because of this celebration, Jewish people from all over had come to Jerusalem to worship.

That was the day God picked to send the Holy Spirit upon the disciples and those followers of Jesus who had gathered together.

This was an observable event. They could hear the sound from heaven, like a rushing mighty wind. They could see the tongues of fire that rested on them. It could not be mistaken for anything but a direct act of Almighty God. This was what Jesus had promised!

How did the Spirit of God make such a change in their lives? What were the changes? We see three changes that were evident.

They were able to speak languages they had not known.

Many missionaries today have to go through a grueling process before going to their field of service. This is called language school. They have to be able to communicate in a meaningful way to the people they want to reach.

I had a professor in Bible College that was a retired missionary. He told us that his first missionary assignment was to a group of people who did not speak English. He spent a great deal of time studying their language. At last, he felt he was ready to preach to them in their own language.

His subject was the bronze serpent that Moses was instructed to put on a pole so that anyone who was bitten could look at the bronze snake and he would live. He made the statement (or so he thought), "The snakes bit the people." Everyone laughed. He said it again and everyone laughed. He asked them what he had said that was so funny. They told him that he'd said, "The people bit the snakes!"

On the day of Pentecost, God wanted the crowds who were present to hear about forgiveness of sin and hear about a living Savior. He made sure that the tongues that these Christians were speaking were languages that the people would recognize. The disciples didn't know all these different languages, so God took control of the situation in this unique way.

They were able to understand the Old Testament scriptures.

Remember the two disciples on their way home to Emmaus? They didn't understand that the Old Testament was talking about Jesus. It was not until Jesus explained it to them that their hearts "burned within them."

Neither did the religious leaders understand the scriptures. They were very familiar with God's Word, but yet did not apply it to Jesus. They had spent many hours memorizing it and debating it. Yet they had no understanding of God's overall plan.

Now we see that after the Holy Spirit comes upon them, things are different. Peter takes a text from the prophet, Joel, and relates it to what was going on at the moment. That passage spoke about God sending His Spirit to dwell in many people.

Sometime later, Stephen, the first Christian martyr, was able to give a history of God's relationship with the people He loved – the descendants of Abraham – and relate it to the present time.

Jesus promised His disciples that the Holy Spirit would give them spiritual understanding. John 14:26 says, *"But the Helper, the Holy Spirit, whom the Father will send in My name, He will teach you all things and bring to your remembrance all that I have said to you."* Peter's sermon was evidence of that promise.

They were able to do miracles.

After the Spirit had come, Peter preached to the crowd. 3,000 people were saved! What happened to those people? Did they go on about their business, just as before? By no means!

Acts 2:42 & 43 tells us something about the life of the early church. They studied together. They ate together. They worshipped together. Verse 43 says, *"Everyone was filled with awe, and may wonders and miraculous signs were done by the apostles."*

This brings us to Acts, Chapter 3, which tells us about one of the miracles.

GOD USED THE APOSTLES TO ACCOMPLISH HIS PURPOSE.

Peter and John still followed many of the Jewish customs. They went to the temple at the time of the evening sacrifice. As they were about to enter the temple courts, they encountered a beggar. He was a beggar because he was lame. He had never taken a step in his life! Peter healed the man in the name of Jesus. This drew a crowd and Peter preached the gospel to them. This aroused the anger of the Jewish religious leaders. They imprisoned Peter and John and warned them not to preach in Jesus' name anymore. We can see four things in this story.

The power that comes in the name of Jesus.

Jesus had told His disciples earlier that they could do nothing apart from Him. (John 15:5) Only as they followed the Spirit's leading and were faithful to Christ, could they do anything.

The lame man asked them for money, but Peter wanted to do so much more for him. He wanted to change this man's life completely. Therefore, he told the man, *"...In the name of Jesus Christ of Nazareth, walk."* (Acts 3:6)

When the crowd gathered to see this miraculous healing, Peter let them know it was not by their own power that this had happened. Later, when questioned by the Jewish priests, Peter gave the credit to the power of Christ.

The joy of the man that was healed.

When Christ comes into a life, the result is joy. This man, who had never walked, all of a sudden began to walk. Then he jumped! Then he praised God!

When I entrusted my life to Christ and accepted Him as Savior and Lord, I, too, was filled with joy. Although I could walk just fine, I knew I was changed on the inside. I still remember it like it was yesterday, although it was over fifty years ago. I knew that my sins were forgiven and I finally understood what the cross was all about.

The amazement of the crowd.

There were many people there that day. This was a special time of day at the temple. While the priests were the ones who made the sacrifices, it was customary for the people to gather together in the outer court and pray.

Many came day after day and were used to seeing the beggar at the gate. He was like a permanent fixture. He sat there day after day.

Suddenly, this well-known person was doing an unimaginable thing. He was standing! No, he was walking! No, he was jumping! No wonder the crowd was amazed.

Peter used this occasion to tell the crowd about Jesus. He makes the lame to walk, the blind to see, the deaf to hear and the dumb to speak. Greater than all of these, however, Jesus offers forgiveness to even the worst of sinners and sets us on the road to heaven. It is still amazing, today, to see a life that has been turned around by the touch of Jesus.

The hatred of the religious leaders.

Not everybody was happy about this miracle. The religious leaders were upset that a crowd was gathering to hear this "ignorant" preacher. He had not gone through their training program. How dare he address the crowd! What was even worse, he was preaching in the name of Jesus. They had hated the man, and now they hated the name.

Why was it that the very people who spent hour after hour studying, memorizing and debating scripture were the ones who hated Jesus the most?

Maybe it was because they had a lot of knowledge, but were cold-hearted toward others. Perhaps it was that they were comfortable with their way of doing things and they did not want to change. They had their sacrifices and their rituals and that was good enough. The principal reason they hated Jesus so much, was that He told them it wasn't good enough. They wanted Jesus to pat them on the shoulder, and instead, He kicked them in the "gluteus maximus."

There were two main groups that made up the leadership. They were known as Pharisees and Sadducees.

The Sadducees were made up of priests, who had charge of the temple and the sacrifices. They did not believe in angels and they did not believe in life after death. They also differed from the Pharisees in their policy of cooperation with the Roman government.

The Pharisees were known as "separated ones". They were very particular in what they did and did not do. They professed to have a high regard for God's law. The trouble was, they added rules and regulations to the law, so that it became a burden instead of a guideline. This was why they had so many quarrels with Jesus over what could be done on the Sabbath day.

There was also a ruling council of the Jews called the Sanhedrin. This was made up of 70 elders, (Pharisees and Sadducees, both.) This group had great power and authority over Jewish affairs.

They had their own police force. Peter and John were arrested and called before the Sanhedrin the next day. The elders could not deny the miracle, but waned them not to preach or teach in the name of Jesus anymore.

Did this work? Were Peter and John so frightened that they shut up? Absolutely not! They went home to the other disciples and prayed for boldness.

The rest of the book of Acts is the story of how the good news about Jesus spread throughout the Roman empire. As persecution increased, boldness increased. The more problems there were, the more faith was evident.

The story has not stopped. It has come down through the ages and now rests upon our shoulders. Let God use you for His purpose!

You may be asking yourself, "How can God use me? I'm just one little individual with limited talents, knowledge and ability." Good question! The answer – God's plan is for you to join with other people of limited talents, knowledge and ability. This can be done by joining a church. Through people working together, God can use whatever ability you have and join it to someone else's ability and someone else's talent to bring forth a result that will bring glory to Him.

Everywhere the apostles went, they started churches. The idea was for like-minded people to get together to strengthen each other, encourage each other and love each other.

The books following the book of acts are examples of letters written to specific churches and individual Christian leaders. They give us a glimpse of early day church life and how people can glorify God by working together to promote His kingdom.

Chapter 16

"ON THIS ROCK I WILL BUILD MY~ CHURCH"

Matthew 16:18 "And I tell you that you are Peter, and on this rock, I will build my church, and the gates of Hades will not overcome it."

Ephesians 4:11 & 12 "It was He who gave some to be apostles, some to be prophets, some to be evangelists and some to be pastors and teachers, to prepare God's people for works of service, so that the body of Christ may be built up."

My dad's father kept a diary and was in the habit of writing down two things for each day – the weather and his activities during the day. It did not take me very long to find out that his favorite things in life were writing letters and receiving letters.

My mother was the same way. She would write long detailed letters to us after we left home. She always complained that we didn't write back often enough.

The apostle Paul was a man my mother would have loved to have for a son. Now, there was a letter-writer, if there ever was one. There were years in Paul's ministry in which he was not free to go where he wanted to go. If he couldn't visit a church, he wrote a letter.

The books between the book of Acts and the book of Revelation are called the Epistles. Most of them were written by Paul, although Peter wrote two short ones and the apostle John wrote three letters. The others were James and Jude.

An epistle is nothing more than a letter. These letters show the depths of the writers' emotions. They were written to encourage, rebuke and instruct. They are written to individuals as well as to churches.

LETTERS OF ENCOURAGEMENT

On Paul's second missionary journey, he encountered a young man named Timothy who was a believer. When Paul and Silas left the area for other towns, Timothy went with them as their helper.

Timothy acted in several capacities in Paul's ministry. Sometimes he was a companion who was actively involved. Sometimes he was a representative. When Paul could not go somewhere himself, he would send Timothy.

By the time the letter known as 1st Timothy was written, we find that Timothy was the pastor of the church in Ephesus. We see the deep love between these two men as Paul writes to encourage his young friend.

The books in the Bible known as 1st and 2nd Timothy are letters of encouragement. Perhaps we can find some encouragement for ourselves.

Paul reminded Timothy of his past.

1st Timothy 1:18 says, *"Timothy, my son, I give you this instruction in keeping with the prophecies once made about you, so that by following them you may fight the good fight, holding on to faith and a good conscience."*

Apparently, when Timothy came to faith in Christ, there were some people who saw some spiritual qualities in him that impressed them. They knew he was destined to be used greatly by God.

Later, in 2nd Timothy, Paul reminded Timothy of his spiritual upbringing. His grandmother was a believer. His mother was a believer. Their faith impacted his life. He made his own decision about salvation, but his decision was influenced by their godly lives.

Paul reminded Timothy of God's power.

Being the pastor of a church is not a job for the faint-hearted. We conclude from some of the things Paul said that Timothy was somewhat timid, was somewhat sickly and was somewhat inexperienced.

2nd Timothy 1:7 says, *"For God did not give us a spirit of timidity, but a spirit of power, of love and of self-discipline."*

When we get to the place where we are aware of our weaknesses, let us remember that God has given us His Spirit and His strength to compensate for our weakness.

LETTERS OF REBUKE

Paul was not timid about condemning wrongdoing in the Christian life.

Rebuking false doctrine

One of Paul's letters that is sterner in tone than some of the others is the letter to the Galatians. Usually, Paul starts his letter with a warm greeting, then assures them of his love and prayers for them. There may be a rebuke somewhere in the letters, but he usually starts with compliments rather than condemnation. In the book of Galatians, however, Paul gives a very short greeting. He then gets right to the heart of the problem they were facing.

The problem was that they had received new life in Christ, but some people had come along and convinced them they had to follow all the Jewish laws and customs in order to maintain a right relationship with God. It was as if someone gave you a free gift, then told you that you had to pay them $20 a week to keep that gift. If you have to pay, it is not a gift.

This is the idea behind God's gift of salvation. You can't earn it. You don't deserve it. All you can do is accept it. We are saved through God's grace by faith plus nothing else. See Ephesians 2:8.

Rebuking bad behavior.

In the book of 1st Corinthians, Paul rebukes bad behavior. One of the church members was having an affair with his stepmother. The other church members were treating it as no big deal. Paul says they should be grieved by it and not take it lightly.

One of his harshest rebukes was for their abuse of the Lord's supper. In 1st Corinthians 11:17-34 Paul tells them they are doing more harm than good by their behavior.

Evidently, the unleavened bread and the wine that constituted the Lord's supper was accompanied by a potluck dinner. The rich members of the church were not waiting for the poor. They were eating too much and drinking too much.

The emphasis of the Lord's supper was a solemn reminder of Jesus' sacrifice and His promise to come again. They were missing the whole point.

LETTERS OF INSTRUCTION

Any appliance or machine you buy comes with an instruction book. You need to know how to use what you have purchased. The same is true of the Christian life. The Bible is our instruction book.

Most of Paul's letters can be broken down into two categories. One of the sections is about **what** God has given us. The other is about how to **use** what God has given us. The book of Ephesians is a good example of this.

Instruction about WHAT God has given us

In Ephesians, chapter 1, we find that God has blessed us with all spiritual blessings in the heavenly places. He has given us hope, He has given us riches and He has given us power.

In chapter 2, we see the great difference that God has made in our lives. He has brought us from death to life. He has raised us up with Christ. He has prepared a job for us to do.

Chapter 3 talks about the privilege we now have to approach God in prayer.

Instruction on how to USE what God has given us

Chapters 4 through 6 of Ephesians tell us what these changes in our lives should look like in our day-to-day living.

We need to act toward our Christian brothers and sisters with humility. Pride is the cause of many a church split. God is grieved when His kids bicker and quarrel.

We need to change our way of life. We need to take off our old way of living and put on the new clothing God has provided. Ephesians 4:22-24 says, *"You were taught, with regard to your former way of life, to put off your old self, which is being corrupted by its deceitful desires; to be made new in the attitude of your minds; and to put on the new self, created to be like God in true righteousness and holiness."*

Chapter 6 tells us our family relationships should be different because of Christ.

Summing up, being a Christian should impact every area of our life. It should make us a better employee or boss. It should make us a better parent. It should make us a better spouse.

How are you putting into practice the gifts that God has given to you?

Chapter 17

GOD WINS!

Revelation 1:1-3 "The revelation of Jesus Christ, which God gave Him to show His servants what must soon take place. He made it known by sending His angel to His servant John, who testifies to everything he saw – that is, the word of God and the testimony of Jesus Christ. Blessed is the one who reads the words of this prophecy, and blessed are those who hear it and take to heart what is written in it, because the time is near."

Revelation 1:12-16 " I turned around to see the voice that was speaking to me. And when I turned, I saw seven golden lampstands, and among the lampstands was someone 'like a son of man,' dressed in a robe reaching down to his feet and with a golden sash around his chest. His head and hair were white like wool, as white as snow, and his eyes were like blazing fire. His feet were like bronze glowing in a furnace, and His voice was like the sound of rushing waters. In His right hand He held seven stars, and out of His mouth came a sharp double-edged sword. His face was like the sun shining in all its brilliance."

The book of Revelation is a scary and mysterious book to a lot of people. If you are not a Christian it **should** be scary. If you are a Christian, though, it should not scare you. It should be a cause of rejoicing that God is indeed going to do away with sin.

There is a lot of figurative language in the book There is a lot of disagreement about how to interpret things. Enough books have been written about Revelation to kill a forest. It is not my purpose in these brief pages to answer all questions. My purpose is to give a general overview of the things God will do at the end of time.

THE AUTHORITY OF THE MESSAGE - FROM JESUS CHRIST, HIMSELF

Many times, in the past, God sent an angel to give a specific message to someone. An angel gave an interpretation to Daniel. An angel told Manoah and his wife that they were to have a son in their

old age. The prophet, Zechariah, had many visions which an angel explained to him.

In this case, an angel was involved, but the message came from the Lord Jesus, Himself.   Let us see how He is described. He was described as:

He is the first and the last.

John 1:1 says that when creation began, Jesus was already there. He had been at the Father's side from eternity past. He is there today and will be there for eternity in the future.

He who was once dead is now alive.

There were many great miracles associated with the life of Jesus, but the greatest miracle was the resurrection. Jesus told His disciples many times that He would be betrayed, arrested and killed. He also told them, however, that three days later He would rise from the dead.

This was the proof that Jesus was really who He said He was. Death does not defeat God – even the God who became a human being. Death is only temporary. Life is forever.

He holds the keys of death and Hell.

In John 14:6 Jesus declares, *"I am the way, the truth and the life. No one comes unto the Father but by me.*

He is the revealer of mysteries.

The risen Jesus walked along with the two men on their way home to Emmaus after that terrible Friday of the crucifixion. Luke 24:25-27 says, *"He said to them, 'How foolish you are and how slow of heart to believe all that the prophets have spoken! Did not the Christ have to suffer these things and then enter His glory?' And beginning with Moses and all the prophets He explained to them what was said in all the Scriptures concerning Himself."*

To be sure, God never played "hide and seek" with mankind. He has always revealed Himself throughout history. From walking with

Adam and Eve in the garden to speaking directly to individuals, God has made Himself known.

He spoke to Noah. He spoke to Abraham, Isaac, and Jacob. He gave them promises. Later He revealed Himself to Moses and, through Moses, to the descendants of Jacob – the nation of Israel.

Although God revealed Himself in these ways, there were still great gaps in the knowledge of God's overall plan. Jesus told His disciples that He would send them the Holy Spirit. That Spirit would help them understand the truth.

There are still mysteries that have not been revealed to us. In John's vision of future events, there were many things he did not understand. There were some things that were revealed to him and others that were not.

One of the things that was never revealed was, "When is all this going to happen?" When asked that very question, Jesus answered that even He did not know. It was simply going to happen when God said it would. There have been foolish people down through history who have set a date for the return of Christ and have been proved wrong.

The point is, we don't have to know when. The closer we get to Jesus, the more we will understand God's overall plan. All we really need to know is that God is in control.

THE LETTERS TO THE SEVEN CHURCHES

There were certainly more than seven churches in the world. Why did Christ pick these seven? It may have been that these particular churches had a great influence on their communities.

To the church in Ephesus Jesus reveals Himself as the head of the church. He is not an absentee landlord. He commends them for their hard work and perseverance. The problem was, they were doing "church" out of habit and there was a lack of genuine love for Him.

The church in Smyrna is commended and there is no rebuke. Instead, they are warned of coming persecution and promised comfort and strength in the midst of their trials.,

The church in Pergamum is commended for their faithfulness. Their rebuke is that they tolerated people who taught that it is alright for a Christian to practice immorality. In other words, it not only matters what WE believe. We are not to have false teachers in our church who teach something different.

The church in Thyatira is in the same situation. So, what is Jesus saying? Is He saying that everyone in the church has to agree on every minor detail of doctrine and belief? No! He is saying that the Christian is held to a higher standard because they belong to Christ. Our family was known in our hometown for its integrity and honesty. Because I was part of the family, I was expected to act in the same way. There is a time, as a Christian, to stand firmly for the truth.

The church in Sardis is not pleasing to Christ because He has not found their deeds complete. There may have been a great deal of activity but there was little love for God and respect for His standards.

There is no rebuke for the church in Philadelphia. Christ commends them for their hard work and their steadfastness. He promises them relief from the time of trial that is coming upon them. This is an important point for us to remember. He does not stop trials from coming our way, but He will give us strength to endure them.

The saddest message is the one to the church at Laodicea. Jesus' message to this church is basically, "You make me sick!" This church was facing no persecution. This church didn't have the problem of false teachers. The problem was their "ho-hum" attitude toward the Savior. They were just going through the motions of worship. If you go to church and your heart has not been changed, you haven't worshipped.

Chapters 4 & 5 reveal the holiness of God and the worthiness of Christ. Chapters 6-16 talk about the judgment of God upon sin.

JUDGMENT UPON SIN

This judgment is not because God has thrown a temper tantrum. This judgment is designed to get men to repent of sin, but they refuse. Each judgment is more severe than the previous one.

Seven seals are broken.

At the time that John was writing these things, it was common to seal a letter by applying a bit of wax. It was an effective way of insuring privacy. If the seal was broken, you knew that someone had tampered with the letter.

In this case, there was not one seal, but seven seals. Why does the number seven appear so much? Seven is the number of completion. Seven is God's number. That is why the number 666 is significant. Six is man's number and it always falls short of God's number.

In the following chapters of Revelation, we see the completeness of God's judgment on sin.

As the first seal is broken, the rider on the white horse is allowed to achieve a military victory. We can see from these judgments that they were **allowed** by God. This conqueror probably does not give God any credit. He may think he has conquered by his own wisdom or strength. Nevertheless, the lesson of the Bible is that God raises up rulers for His purpose.

The rider on the second horse was given power to take peace from the earth and to make men kill each other.

The third judgment was a natural consequence of the previous one. In the face of such devastation, famine was widespread. It became so bad that a person had to work all day to get enough for a meal.

The fourth rider was "death", followed by "Hades". We have seen and heard of vast numbers of people being killed, but this is so bad that a quarter of the earth's population is killed.

The fifth seal reveals a different picture. The people who had been martyred for being Christians are calling for God's judgment on sin. They are comforted and told to wait a little while longer.

As the sixth seal was broken there was a great earthquake, the sun was darkened and the stars fell from the sky. The sky receded like a scroll being rolled up and mountains and islands were removed from their place.

The seventh seal prepared the way for seven more judgments.

Seven trumpets are blown.

Trumpets were very important in Jewish life. Along with the ten commandments and the instructions for the tabernacle, Moses was instructed to have two silver trumpets made. These trumpets were to be used to call an assembly, used in war and used at special feast days during the year. We find that besides these silver trumpets, there were trumpets made of ram's horns. This is the trumpet called the "shofar."

Rev. 8:7 says, *"The first angel sounded his trumpet and hail and fire mixed with blood was hurled down upon the earth. A third of the earth was burned up, a third of the trees and all the green grass was burned up."*

In one of the earlier judgments, we saw that a fourth of earth's population has been killed. At this time one third of the earth is affected. God's wrath against sin is getting more severe.

The second angel sounded his trumpet and John tried to describe something which he had never seen and tried to make it understandable to his readers. "A huge mountain thrown into the sea," was the best explanation he could come up with. Whatever it was affected the sea. A third of the sea turned into blood, a third of ships were destroyed, and a third of sea creatures died.

At the next trumpet, a third of the fresh water supply became undrinkable. As bad as these things were, we can still see the mercy of God. One third was affected but two thirds were not.

The fourth judgment affected the sun, moon and stars. As we consider these things, we see that now not only is the earth affected. The lights that God designed to rule the day and the night were being affected.

Trumpet number five of this series brings forth a special swarm of locusts that God has kept reserved especially for this particular time. These locusts are unlike any we've ever seen. Instead of eating vegetation, they are given the power to torment people with their stings. These stings will be so painful that people will long to die, but cannot.

By this time, you might think that the people left on earth might begin to get serious about their relationship with God. Not so! Rev. 9:20 and 21 says, *"The rest of mankind that were not killed by these plagues still did not repent of the work of their hands; they did not stop worshipping demons, and idols of gold, silver, bronze, stone and wood – idols that cannot see or hear or walk. Nor did they repent of their murders, their magic arts, their sexual immorality or their thefts."*

The sixth trumpet results in the death of one third of mankind.

The seventh trumpet brings on an earthquake and a hailstorm.

Seven bowls are poured out.

The last seven plagues are represented by bowlfuls of God's wrath being poured out.

The first bowl results in ugly and painful sores upon people – but not all people. The sores come up on only those who worship the antichrist – those who have taken his mark upon them, the mark of 666.

The second angel poured out his bowl and the entire sea turned to blood. We have seen before, at the sounding of the second trumpet, how one third of the sea was turned to blood. A third of the sea creatures died and a third of the ships were destroyed. At this time the entire marine life was destroyed.

The third bowl was poured out upon the fresh water supply and all the water became blood.

The fourth judgment affected the sun. How did God do that? Did He crank up the heat a few degrees? Maybe He just moved it a few inches closer to earth. The important thing was not how it was done, but that it WAS done.

See the outcome of this plague. Instead of driving people to repent, it hardened them in their sin. Instead of turning to God in repentance, they turned away from Him in rebellion. See Rev. 16:9

The fifth bowl brought utter darkness. The attitude of people remained the same. They cursed God and went on in their sin.

The sixth bowl was poured out and the Euphrates river was dried up. This may not seem to us like such a bad thing. But it prepared the way for God's enemies to gather together for a final battle against Him.

The seventh bowl was accompanied by a voice from the throne in heaven saying, "It is done!" It brought an earthquake so great that the Richter scale couldn't even begin to register it. There were also hailstones of about one hundred pounds.

The eighth bowl – WAIT A MINUTE! There was no eighth bowl. God had brought an end to His judgment. Seven seals. Seven trumpets. Seven bowls. 777 – God's perfect number.

ALL THINGS NEW

Although the majority of mankind has held out against God to the end, He has the last word. Satan is defeated and sin is punished. Now the good news. God can start over again, now that sin is done away with. This is the subject of Revelation chapters 21 and 22.

There is a new heaven and a new earth.

Revelation 21:1 says, *"Then I saw a new heaven and a new earth, for the first heaven and the first earth had passed away, and there was no more sea."* The apostle Peter said the same thing in his second letter of encouragement to Christians. II Peter 3:11-13 talks about this very thing. God promised Noah that He would never destroy the earth with a flood again. We see here that it won't be a flood. It will be a fire.

There is a new Jerusalem.

The city of Jerusalem was of extreme importance to the Jewish people. King David set up his headquarters in Jerusalem. See 2nd

Samuel 5:5. Jerusalem was the home of the magnificent temple built by Solomon. The people from all over Israel came to Jerusalem for the festivals.

Now God has made a new Jerusalem according to His own specifications. See Revelation 21:9-21 for a description of that city. The foundations honor Jesus' apostles. The gates bear the names of the tribes of Israel.

There is a new relationship with God, Himself.

Although I have had a relationship with God since I was 24 years old, it is a relationship that is based on faith. The disciple, Thomas, believed the resurrection when he actually saw Jesus standing before him. John 20:29 says, *"Then Jesus told him, 'Because you have seen me, you have believed; blessed are those who have not seen and yet have believed."* I have experienced the joy that comes from having a relationship with the Lord. I have had the blessing of being led by God, being used by God and being forgiven by Him. But I have never seen Him. All that will change in the future.

HOW CAN I GET THERE?

The Bible says that we, as people have a problem. That problem is sin. Romans 3:23 says, *"for all have sinned and fall short of the glory of God."* Yet, God Knows about our sin and has made provision for that sin. Romans 6:23 says, *"For the wages of sin is death, but the gift of God is eternal life in Christ Jesus our Lord."* When we consider these things, we can see that entering into a relationship with God is as simple as ABC.

A-Attitude

There must be a new attitude toward sin. We tend to excuse our sin or minimize it or ignore it. Before we can receive the gift of eternal like we need to come to the place of realizing that we have offended a holy God.

There were many people who came to John the Baptist. John would not baptize any that would not repent of their sin. He saw that those that were the most religious were basing their standing before God on the good things they had done and the religion they were born into. John told them, *"...you brood of vipers! Who warned you to flee from the coming wrath? Produce fruit in keeping with repentance. And do not begin to say to yourselves, 'We have Abraham as our father.' For I tell you that out of these stones God can raise up children for Abraham."* *Luke 3: 7 & 8.* John then went on to tell them some specific ways their repentance should show up in their everyday life.

In short, you can't be a Christian gangster. You need to be willing to turn away from your sin. This is repentance – a change of direction. Instead of running away from God you are turning toward Him.

B-Belief

Hebrews 11:1 describes what faith is. It says, *"Now faith is being sure of what we hope for and certain of what we do not see."* Going on a little further in the chapter, verse 6 describes how necessary faith is. It states, *"And without faith it is impossible to please God, because anyone who comes to him must believe that He exists and that He rewards those who earnestly seek Him."* We might well have a desire to turn away from our sin, but without faith we will never come to the source of forgiveness.

So, what do we have to believe? First of all, we must believe that Jesus is really God. There are some religions in the world that have a high regard for Jesus, but do not believe that He was God. If you find a church like that – don't join it! The first chapter of the gospel of John makes the case very clear.

Second, we must believe that Jesus died on the cross as a substitute for us. Instead of having to die because we are guilty, Jesus paid the penalty so God could freely forgive our sin. Only Jesus could do this because He had no sin of His own to pay for.

Third, we must believe that Jesus is the only way to heaven. Jesus was talking to His disciples on His last night on earth. John 14:4-6 says, *"You know the way to the place I am going. Thomas said to Him, 'Lord, we don't know where You are going, so how can we know the way?' Jesus answered, 'I am the way and the truth and the life. No one comes to the Father except through Me.'"* There are many things in the Bible that puzzle me, but that declaration from the Savior could not be more clear or certain.

C-Call upon Jesus.

So far, so good. You have a desire to turn away from sin. You have the right belief about who Jesus is and what He has done for You. What is the only thing missing? Simply this – you have to call.

During His time on earth, Jesus never went where He was not wanted. After He healed the man who had many demons, the people of the region, in spite of the miracle, asked Him to leave. Instead of arguing with them or resisting their will, He simply got in the boat and left.

God has given us free will for a reason. He will enter anyone's life if He is invited. He leaves it up to us, though, to issue the invitation. Revelation 3: 20 says, *"Here I am! I stand at the door and knock. If anyone hears my voice and opens the door, I will come in and eat with him and he with Me."* There can be only two responses. "Jesus, come in!" or "Jesus, stay out!"

I volunteer at a local elementary school. Once in a while a child will come to the teacher in tears, telling about how they were mistreated by a classmate. Usually, the teacher will respond, "Did you tell Johnny how you felt about that and ask him to stop?" If the answer is "no", the teacher will say, "Use your words."

That is what God wants us to do. He wants us to use our words. We can use our words to tell Him how much we love Him. We can use our words to invite Him into our lives. We can use our words to tell others of the great and glorious God we serve. USE YOUR WORDS!!!

Chapter 18

CONCLUSIONS

Now we have come to the last book in God's library. We see that in spite of man's sin and rebellion, God wins. What conclusions can we draw as we have seen God's activity in human affairs, down through the ages?

One conclusion is surely this – God created mankind for fellowship with Him and placed Him in a perfect environment. We can also conclude that in spite of sin, forgiveness was available.

We have also seen that God rewards faithfulness, as seen in the life of Abraham. Abraham followed God, worshipped God and believed God.

God gave certain promises to Abraham. He promised him many descendants and a land of their own. He passed those promises down to Abraham's son, Isaac and then to Isaac's son, Jacob. It did not look hopeful for Jacob's descendants. They were in slavery in the land of Egypt. Had God changed His mind? Had He forgotten about hose promises? Absolutely not! He was just waiting for the right time.

Finally, at just the right time God used Moses to deliver His people from slavery. Keep in mind, however, that although God USED Moses, it was God, Himself, who was behind the events. After God got His people out of Egypt, He took them out into the desert with the intent of getting "Egypt" out of them!

He made a covenant with the whole nation of Israel at Mount Sinai. He gave them laws to live by. He gave them a system of worship. He had them build a tabernacle so He could dwell among them.

You would think that after seeing God's power demonstrated again and again both in the land of Egypt and the miraculous provision for them in the desert, there would not be a problem with trusting God. Not so! The people refused the land God wanted to give them because

they heard there were giants in the land. Alas, they were condemned to wandering in the wilderness for 40 years.

God's plan was till in action, though. The next generation got a chance to receive God's blessings that their parents refused. They had a new leader – Joshua. They conquered a new land. At the end of his life, Joshua pleaded with the people to maintain their love for the Lord.

After many years of being without a king, the people wanted a king "like all the other nations." God gave them what they wanted, but the first king turned away from God and God rejected him. This time God chose a man whose heart would be loyal to Him. The second king – David – was chosen at an early age, empowered by God to defeat Goliath, and protected from the rage of King Saul, who thought he was still in charge. Toward the end of David's life, God made a covenant with him concerning his descendants. One of those descendants is none other than our Lord Jesus Christ.

We have seen the love of God displayed as He took the descendants of Abraham, Isaac and Jacob and made them into a nation. He gave them a land of their own, as He had promised. Their occupation of that land and their enjoyment of its blessings were conditional on obedience.

Part of love is discipline. A father can give his teenage son a car, but if he uses it irresponsibly, the father can take the keys away. The car still belongs to the son, but he can't use it until he straightens up.

God is a perfect parent and knows when to administer discipline. He warned His people, through Moses, that obedience brings blessing and disobedience is costly to you and those around you. Deuteronomy 28 spells out the consequences of obedience and disobedience in great detail.

God allowed foreign nations to conquer His people. After that discipline, however,

God restored His people and allowed them to move back to the land He had given them.

Up until this time, God had sent prophet after prophet to warn his people and encourage them. Even after they returned to the land there were prophets. Finally, He stopped sending them. It was as if He said, "If you're not going to listen, why should I talk to you?" There was a period when God was silent for over 350 years.

Finally, God sent another prophet – John the Baptist - to announce the great news that God's son had come to earth as a human being to take care of our sin problem. John chapter 1 talks about the Word (which Jesus was called,) the witness to the Word, and the world's reaction to that Word.

After spending three years with His disciples, Jesus gave them a test. He wanted to know if they really realized who He was. Peter gave the answer (for all the disciples) that He was the Son of the living God. It is not enough just to know who Jesus is. You must take the next step and invite Him to share your life.

The crucifixion was horrifying and gruesome, but it was only the first part of the story. It was a shameful death, but a glorious resurrection. When the women came to anoint the body of Jesus, there was no body! To prove He was really alive, He appeared to His disciples over a period of the next forty days.

The book of Acts records how God accomplished His work through a group of ordinary men who were filled with God's Holy Spirit. There were incredible numbers of people who were brought to the Savior. Jesus was not here on earth, but the work went on.

Finally, we've seen how it will end. Sin will be judged and we will enjoy perfect fellowship with God and with each other.

In view of these things that God has brought about, what should our response be? Should we sit down on the couch, eat potato chips, watch TV and wait for life to play itself out? Well, that would be one way to handle it, but probably not the best way.

Instead, we ought to take seriously the advice of Peter in 2nd Peter 3:11-14. *"Since everything will be destroyed in this way, what kind of people ought you to be? You ought to live holy and godly lives as you look forward to the day of God and speed its coming. That day will bring about the destruction of the heavens by fire, and the elements will melt in the heat. But in keeping with His promise, we are looking forward to a new heaven and a new earth, the home of righteousness. So then, dear friends, since you are looking forward to this, make every effort to be found spotless, blameless and at peace with Him."*

Three admonitions are in order to live a fruitful, enjoyable relationship with the living God.

1. Enjoy the life God has given you.

2. Cooperate with Him in His desire to use you in His service.

3. Rest secure in the knowledge that He is in charge.

ABOUT THE AUTHOR

Kenneth L. Sherlock was born and raised in Lander, Wyoming. After graduating from high school in Lander, Ken attended Utah State University in Logan, Utah for a couple of years. In 1972 he enrolled in Faith Baptist Bible College in Ankeny, Iowa. He graduated from there in 1974 with a B.A. in Bible and Theology.

He married Dona Kenyon on Nov. 13, 1983 in Billings, Montana. They have lived in Billings ever since. Ken has served as pastor and associate pastor for churches in Billings. He was chaplain at "Passages" (a pre-release center for women prisoners) for 12 years.